CW00664458

God the Child

God the Child

Small, weak and curious subversions

Graham Adams

scm press

© Graham Adams 2024

Published in 2024 by SCM Press
Editorial office
3rd Floor, Invicta House,
110 Golden Lane
London EC1Y 0TG, UK

www.scmpress.co.uk

SCM Press is an imprint of Hymns Ancient & Modern Ltd
(a registered charity)

H
Y Ancient
M
N &Modern
S

Hymns Ancient & Modern® is a registered trademark of
Hymns Ancient & Modern Ltd
13A Hellesdon Park Road, Norwich,
Norfolk NR6 5DR, UK

Permission is granted by the author and publisher for the hymns to
be used in non-commercial group performance and accompanying
printed hymn and service sheets. Due acknowledgement must be
made to this book as the source publication. For all other material, all
rights reserved. No part of this publication may be reproduced, stored
in a retrieval system, or transmitted, in any form or by any means,
electronic, mechanical, photocopying or otherwise, without the prior
permission of the publisher, SCM Press.

Graham Adams has asserted his right under the Copyright, Designs
and Patents Act 1988 to be identified as the Author of this Work

Scripture quotations are from New Revised Standard Version Bible:
Anglicized Edition, copyright © 1989, 1995 National Council of the
Churches of Christ in the United States of America. Used by permission.
All rights reserved worldwide.

British Library Cataloguing in Publication data

A catalogue record for this book is available
from the British Library

ISBN 978-0-334-06500-5

Typeset by Regent Typesetting
Printed and bound in Great Britain by
CPI Group (UK) Ltd

Contents

To the child who seems invisible,
whose pain is minimized,
whose silence has so much to tell us,
and who sees what adults dare not see;
the child within us, bewildered but curious,
the child beside us, defiantly not one-dimensional,
the child ahead of us, beckoning us to follow
and imagining the future differently.

Acknowledgements

I wasn't expecting to write this book. It sprung up on me. Before my previous book, *Holy Anarchy*, was published, it dawned on me that this small element within it would particularly benefit from further exploration and growth: why God the Child? So I'm hugely grateful for the people around me who encouraged me and gave me the space to bring this unplanned *God the Child* to birth:

- at SCM: David Shervington, for receiving the idea so positively, and the whole team including Mary Matthews and Linda Crosby;

- at Luther King Centre: in particular Noel Irwin, for helping me to sketch out ideas on the back of an envelope during a retreat when we were supposed to be focusing on something else, and drawing my attention to childlikeness in Paulo Freire; Kim Wasey, for constant encouragement and reading through some of the material at a crucial stage of self-doubt; and everyone's meaningful support, including every colleague who humoured, and therefore enabled, my attempts at playfulness;

- as fellow travellers: Janet Lees and Bob Warwicker, for reading the chapters as they emerged from the shadows;

- for the Foreword: many thanks to Karen O'Donnell, for helpfully and generously situating the project in a wider and longer tradition of anti-idolatry and anti-patriarchy, and for highlighting the playfulness and politics of God the Child;

- at home: unending gratitude to Sheryl, for making it possible for me to give time to this, and for inspiring me with her passion for holistic child-centred education in the midst of systems that make it harder; and Bethan, our daughter, for her creativity and wit, and one of the answers to the question above.

Foreword

Speaking about God Rightly

KAREN O'DONNELL

The ongoing and impossible task of theology is to find ways to speak about God rightly. In the 1990s, this was the task before the feminist theologian Elizabeth Johnson. She explored the questions of whether the reality of women could provide a suitable metaphor for speech about God in her book *She Who Is: The Mystery of God in Feminist Theological Discourse*. This new book by Graham Adams, *God the Child*, is – from my theological perspective – a direct descendant of Johnson's work in the best possible way. As Johnson did, Adams explores how the symbols and metaphors we use for God function, and the impact they have on our theological imaginations.

Johnson was passionately convinced of the need for such work. She wrote: 'What is at stake is the truth about God, inseparable from the situation of human beings, and the identity and mission of the faith community itself.'[1] For Johnson, it was the androcentric order of theology that she wanted to challenge, but encompassed within her goal is something of Adams's work. It was the image of ruling *adult* male against which all others – women, children, and those men who did not fit the patriarchal image – were judged and found wanting, found to be less than human, and certainly unworthy of imaging the Divine. Johnson reminds us that: 'Whenever one image or concept of God expands to the horizon thus shutting out others, and whenever this exclusive symbol becomes literalized so that the distance between it and divine reality is collapsed, there an idol comes into being.'[2]

We have made an idol of God the Adult. This image of God has expanded to the horizon and shut out glimpses of other (better?) ways of speaking rightly about God. It has become an exclusive symbol, as Adams makes clear throughout this book. It has become a literalized symbol so that the distance between the adult and the divine reality of God has collapsed. The idol of God the Adult has long been in existence.

What should we expect, though, when the ways of speaking rightly about God have long been determined by the 'giants'? For centuries, these 'giants' – those small, weak and curious subversions who dominate and determine what speaking rightly about God looks and sounds like – have been adult men in Europe and North America. Other voices – voices of women certainly, but voices of many others who were not the 'right kind of person' (adult man?) – have been and continue to be marginalized and silenced. The problem, as Johnson reminds us, is not that this way of speaking about God is wrong, but that when it is used exclusively, literally and patriarchally, such language fails both humans and divine mystery.[3]

In her work on the problems of projection in social doctrines of the Trinity, Karen Kilby is critical of the ways in which theologians project on to God particular understandings of what it means to be human. She writes: 'Projection, then, is particularly problematic in at least some social theories of the Trinity because what is projected onto God is immediately reflected back onto the world, and this reverse doctrine is said to be what is in fact *important* about the doctrine.'[4]

We have been too satisfied with this received projection, with a God that images us. Who are *us*? Those who get to articulate how we speak rightly of God. For me, as a feminist theologian, this *right speaking* imagines a God that exceeds gender while also holding within Her all that is good about gender. I like to refer to Her as Her – this still, sadly, feels liberative and radical. But she is always Mother, Sister (and always an older sister!) and Friend (gendered as feminine). She is always *adult*. What might it mean for me to encounter God my Little Sister? God my Tiny Infant Niece whom I love to hold in my arms, to spoil and adore, and to play silly games with?

I love the idea, then, that God the Child is one who plays with us! I am reminded of the line in Psalm 104 that is describing the seas God has created and just casually notes: 'There is that Leviathan Which You have made to play there' (Ps. 104.26, NKJV). But play is, as Adams makes clear, serious business. It is a political tool, one that exposes dominating norms and then messes with them. I can appreciate this! I'm the irritating aunt who insists on giving my nieces feminist-inspired gifts. The year I was asked to gift my eldest niece dressing-up clothes, I went for 'surgeon with medical kit' rather than Disney Princess. Play disrupts the systems that discriminate.

This playing of God *with* us, alongside us, is a play that seeks to re-imagine the world. Adams depicts God the Child as a chaos-event, and in doing so re-imagines what power means. It is not strength but rather disruption, with potentially uncontainable repercussions. This kind of play has the butterfly effect of toppling empires and bringing liberation. What a gift to our theological imaginations to begin to recognize the ways in which God the Child might help us to see what it means to live out the liberating gospel – the good news – in our world.

Adams reminds us of the gift of the child and in doing so exposes the limitations of the adult in the aim of speaking rightly about God. We are always encountering God according to the limitations of our imaginations. In this vulnerable and playful text, Adams pushes us a little further in expanding our theological imaginations in order that we might aim to speak just a bit more rightly about God. In doing so, we might *play* our part in imagining a just world as we follow God the Child. Adams ends this work with a re-imagined Creed that reads, in part:

We believe in God the Child
Who has faith that is tiny
As small as a mustard seed
But it gets in the cracks
And it takes root

Letting God the Child take root in our theological imaginations might *just* enable us to move mountains.

Dr Karen O'Donnell, Academic Dean,
Westcott House, Cambridge

Notes

1 Elizabeth Johnson, 1997, *She Who Is: The Mystery of God in Feminist Theological Discourse*, New York: Crossroad, p. 6.
2 Johnson, *She Who Is*, p. 39.
3 Johnson, *She Who Is*, p. 33.
4 Karen Kilby, 2000, 'Perichoresis and Projection: Problems with Social Doctrines of the Trinity', *New Blackfriars*, 81(957), October, p. 442. (Italics in the original.)

First Steps

Introducing God the Child

*But the LORD said to Samuel, 'Do not look on his
appearance or on the height of his stature, because I have
rejected him; for the LORD does not see as mortals see;
they look on the outward appearance,
but the LORD looks on the heart.'*
(1 Samuel 16.7)

Beyond God the Adult

Once upon a time ...
It was a land ruled by giants, or perhaps they were average-sized
people who behaved like giants. And at the top of it, in the
heavens, there was a Giant God. A great big GOD. But, crucially, an Adult God. After all, how could it be any other way?
Some people called God 'Father', others called her 'Mother',
but also Judge, King, Shepherd, Midwife and Saviour. All
apparently adult. What else? Some people remembered a time
when everyone thought of God as an Old Man in the Sky, with
an impressive beard, and they at least felt that this was now a
thing of the past – because they understood that God is Spirit,
without shape or form. They understood that all the names
for God are more like pictures, like sketches of what cannot
be seen. It was as though the pictures pointed the people to
features of the Giant God, who was big enough to include them
all. But God was still, always, adult. Well, perhaps not 'always',
because there was a brief episode when God came among the
people *as a child*, though he grew – in strength and wisdom. It
was a celebrated episode, which people recognized as telling
them something about this Giant God: that he willingly took
on the experience of vulnerability, which he continued in his

human adult life too, even to the point of death. A Giant God who became vulnerable.

But it was his vulnerability that had mattered, not his 'childness'. When this human-God walked the earth, he even called God 'Abba', Father or Daddy, so it was obvious that this adult picture of God was meant to be the main one. Always. Of course, it was possible to imagine that even a young adult, or even an old child, can be a parent, so perhaps this Abba could be much younger than most people pictured. But that was the thing about these pictures; they were fuzzy and could be seen in different ways. It was as though they were partly true, but also not quite true; they grasped at something, and caught some of God in their grasp, but much of God slipped through. Many of the people understood the need for many names. It helped the many varied people to feel that God was a little like them, each of them, though it could seem as though God was more like the adults than the children – but at least God was the creator of many kinds of people, of all backgrounds, all situations, all ages. But even so, one thing was hard to escape: God was an Adult.

But then one day ...
Something strange happened. It was hard to explain. There were often moments like this, for many different people – when things were seen differently. And not everyone would want to hear them. But here it was, something strange. It was as though a small crowd gathered, each one saying something, a small part of an emerging picture and, together, a strange new possibility began to fall into place.

What if God is best understood as a child?

It wasn't that this picture should replace all previous pictures. After all, this picture had already been a small part of the wider collection. But somehow, the picture of God as Child had never quite been developed: almost akin to a series of artworks deserving greater attention in themselves.

None of the voices was trying to say: 'The adult may simply be a bit younger than we imagine', like a young shepherd or a young judge or a young king. That wasn't what was happening, because God can't be pictured as a particular age, surely? But some of the children asked, 'How old is God?' And some of the adults said, 'It's a nonsense question', because some of the giants had insisted that God is outside time. And some of the children wondered what that meant, and asked again, 'But how old is God, then?'

Nor was there a voice saying: 'Well, every adult is also simultaneously a child, a child of their own parents', as though even an adult God could also be a child. That couldn't be what the crowd meant because no one created God, did they – as a child with their own (human) parents? Did they? On the other hand, human adults are indeed simultaneously adult and child, because the child that we 'were' remains with us, a real part of who we 'are'; so it could be that God 'the Adult' is also simultaneously 'Child'; yes, that is part of what was being recognized, with metaphors adding to metaphors, each a little selective, each a little un-rounded, but nevertheless contributing to the overall story.

Crucially, it was as though a small crowd was putting three things into words, like three pictures posing questions. First, the sketch of God as Child made some of the people stop and wonder: Do our adult pictures make as much sense as we imagine? The adult images had seemed so normal, so inevitable, and the first glimpse of God as Child seemed so absurd that God's adultness had to be the only option. How could God, the Giant God of the whole universe, be a child? How could it be! But then people started to wonder: Why ...? Why do we think that God as Adult makes sense of these mysteries? Some of the people started to wonder: Is it because the giants in our world prefer the adult pictures? Powerful people are drawn to images of power and strength, as ways of maintaining the world as it is. Are we all encouraged, perhaps implicitly, to hold on to the Adult God, because adults are people who have learned how to live in the world as it is; they have learned to see things as part of the natural order – whereas children are people exploring what the world could be? They have more scope to re-imagine, so such an image of God as Child may open up too many alternative possibilities. Perhaps.

Second, some people noticed that God as Child was a helpful way of holding together some of the things that the human-God had said and done – not only things he said about himself, but things he had shown about the value of childness, and the need to be like children to enter into the new world of God. Could it mean, actually, that this new world calls us to be like children, because the God who shapes it is childlike?

And third, some of the crowd said that although these ideas are playful, they are neither frivolous nor navel-gazing. Sure, they are about seeing God a bit differently; they challenge those of us, of any age, who feel God must be adult, offering another possibility. But that is not all that they do. They are about the world we live in and the world we hope for. They are about the God who helps us to play and dream for something that we don't always see – because in a world of giants, we don't notice what is small. So look, listen and dream.

About the author and things

I know, it's not normal to write about the author when the story is already underway. But I'm part of this land of giants. I walk its streets, breathe its air, live within its assumptions. It shapes how I see things, for better and for worse. Also, I am very much involved with the global community that celebrates the Adult God. I grew up in church, from a child to an adult. And as an adult I felt the call to be a minister of 'the gospel': the good news of God's love, as demonstrated most intensely in the life, death and resurrection of God the Child, not that it had occurred to me to use that name.

I studied theology, notably contextual theology, which seeks to acknowledge that theology always emerges out of particular contexts, especially all manner of contexts 'belittled' by the power of giants in our world: how westernness, Whiteness, maleness and so on tend to dominate theology, whereas contextual theology raises up the seemingly little voices – those of people rendered small but who, in many ways, speak out of various majorities, or at least weighty minorities – among the poor, the Global South, women and many other groups. But looking back, I realize that the context of the explicitly little – 'the child' – was not very present in those studies. It was only later, when I discovered Child theology, that this struck me. After all, it is a discipline that specifically asks what happens to theology when a child is 'in the midst'. But even within this discipline, there is an avenue crying out to be more directly explored, one which that question opens up: How does the child's presence help us to re-conceive God? Child theology tends to focus on the childness of Jesus' disciples – in other words, what it means to follow God the Child, as understood specifically in relation to Jesus, the human-God. It asks about mission, salvation, church, discipleship – but not so much the assumed adultness of God. There are voices pointing us towards the possibility of a more thoroughgoing divine childness, which I discuss shortly, but they generally seem to assume divine adultness as the default that is simply 'suspended' by incarnation – or, at least, that incarnation is the means by which we see the childness of one of the persons of the Triune God. In other words, they say 'God *became* Child', rather than my wondering: First and foremost, what if God *is* Child? Others too have posed this question, and I want to play with it and develop it.

If I am part of this land of giants, in many ways ill-equipped to see through the eyes of a child, what fragments of experience do I bring to this venture, to see what happens when childness is brought to the very question of God, and not only 'the Son', but our broader canvas of the divine life?

My mum used to comment on my imagination as a child, that I could get lost in writing wild stories. And I recognize that in some ways this has stopped, but perhaps in others that it has continued, since the task of ministry and of being a theologian is partly an act of imagination, of telling a wild story.

At my home church, where I grew up, I remember how it was always a child who was asked to read the verses from Mark (10.13–16) at every infant baptism. Sometimes this responsibility fell to me, and I clearly remember the words (from the Good News Bible):

Some people brought children to Jesus, for him to place his hands on them. But the disciples scolded the people. When Jesus saw this, he was angry, and said to his disciples, 'Let the children come to me, and do not stop them, for the kingdom of God belongs to such as these.' Then he took the children in his arms, placed his hands on them, and blessed them.

Actually, I have written out those verses from memory, so this is not the exact words used in the Good News Bible, but it reflects how the seed of *letting the children come* was sown within me.

In ministry in a Congregational church in Manchester, the involvement of children mattered to me – not merely as 'performance' for the entertainment of adults, but their agency, their voice, their disruptiveness. I am quite sure that I did not make everything as child-friendly as it could have been, and there will have been all sorts of compromise – but together, as a church, we sought to create a culture in which children meaningfully belonged. Even now, perhaps 15 years later, one highlight stands out: an act of worship in which our congregation was sitting in a circle of two rows, with the communion table in the middle, and an activity for younger children was at a table placed within the second row. During communion, in which children and adults shared together, at the point that we were about to share the wine, in our individual glasses, there was a pause, because a young child, aged about six or seven, noticed that the leader of the children's activity had been mistakenly overlooked when the glasses were passed round, so he ran to the centre table, took a glass and gave it to her – and we all drank together. What had been broken was made whole by a child.

As for our own family, it took longer than we had imagined to become three of us, so I try to be mindful of the struggles that many experience – whether it is the ache for children, the tragedy of loss, pregnancy loss, disability, illness, and the many assumptions that we live with, in this land of giants; the invasive questions that people ask, the anxieties people face, the silent traumas people bear; so any talk of God the Child cannot be cheap or glib or a supposedly neat resolution of complex pain. In fact, it seeks to engage with the pain, recognizing that children have a long history of bearing more pain than adults often want to admit: the time spent on staircases listening to adult agonies and anger, the crying behind bedroom doors, the bullying, the name-calling, the hunger and neglect, the insecure housing and the violence. Children bear the pain that flows from adults. Perhaps God the Child is all too aware of this, weeping.

In my writing, it has been an emerging theme: first, God the Child appeared in a chapter called 'Doubting Empire', back in 2016, wrestling with the ways in which political structures – but also church assumptions and theologies – view children in a certain way. This is because they implicitly want *adults* to be a certain way as well – acquiescent, present but quiet, faithful to the boundaries set down – whereas God the Child in Christ dares to show a way of disruption, in solidarity with those who doubt, who resist and question, whether absent or present. It became a stronger theme in my book *Holy Anarchy*, a symbol of God's alternative power, awesome weakness, in the midst of and subverting the overbearing power of the Domination System; it is God the Child who shows us, even through small-ness and the generative potential of chaos, the disproportionate transformations that can arise.

I note, however, that Adrian Thatcher also used the term, specifically to argue that children's rights can be rooted in the childhood of Christ.[1] But this is too limited. More comprehensively, Janet Pais suggests 'God is Child', but focuses on Jesus.[2] As Ryan Stollar elaborates, Pais is arguing that the Trinity's parent–child relationship is critical: the 'childness' of the divine is intrinsic to Jesus' identity.[3] It is not, through the incarnation, that God was taking on a new aspect of Godself, but that the eternal reality of divine childness was being revealed.[4] This gives worth to childness, subverting the human projection of worth on to God as Adult.[5] The subversion of God-models is intrinsic to Pais's work as a liberation theologian, seeing God through the experience of the oppressed, in this case children who suffer at the hands of adults – including the experience of child abuse.[6] God as Child becomes the judge of such behaviour, the abuse of a child being the abuse of God; and just as Black or feminist or Queer theologies see God through experiences of oppression, so the suffering and abuse of children enables us to see 'GOD IS CHILD'.[7] Consequently, for Pais, the incarnation reveals to us the childness of God, God's judgement on the adult abuse of children, and the possibility of our restorative relationship with the childness of God.[8] This is, then, an insight into the very life of God with whom we may be in relationship, but essentially focused on the childness, as embodied in Jesus, of the second person of the Trinity: God the Child.

For Stollar, God's 'becoming' a child is crucial – notably 'a powerless, fully human god-child born into a violently anti-child world',[9] the means by which we are reorientated to God's alternative realm, 'the kingdom of children'.[10] Wendy Deifelt, too, sees the 'God-Child paradigm' as being focused on God's 'assuming a child's body',[11] which 'temporarily' changes things,[12] rather than being integral to God's nature as such. She comes close to the possibility of God as Child when discussing the danger of idolizing our images, but her focus is Jesus as child of God.[13] In *Holy Anarchy*, I was not directly challenging these approaches but beginning to point towards a different possibility, if only implicitly: specifically in terms of Jesus as the embodiment of God the Child.[14] In other words, as for Pais, Jesus *makes known* the reality of God as Child, a reality that preceded incarnation. However, for me this possibility does not rely on the internal trinitarian relationships, and the distinctiveness of the 'Second Person', but rather involves a reconfiguring of God, as open palm, chaos-event and horizon-seeker, in each case by way of divine childness.

In other words, it has dawned on me more directly that this is not simply about Jesus, nor the incarnation, but about God more comprehensively. I come back to this discussion in Part 2, particularly in Chapter 4 regarding Jesus, and in Chapter 5 when addressing the debates among different movements in theology that consider the child (including Child Liberation Theology). But, crucially, my approach differs a little, constructing its argument with different building blocks, for I am not as such asking what happens when we see God's childness by virtue of *Jesus having been a child*, nor only when we affirm that *Jesus is God's Child*, or 'the God Child', but when the primary metaphor for God's very being is not an adult temporarily suspended, or a parent-child relationship within itself, but simply a Child.

Of course, the idea of God as Child is still, essentially, in its relative infancy; even as I write this book, I envisage other sightings of the Child at large and I recognize that the notion is indeed in its early stages of development; so this does not pretend to be comprehensive, even as I presume to offer a reconstructive account of the divine life and the implications for church and world.

The five giants supporting the Adult God

I wonder: What are the giants who particularly stand in the way of such an alternative version of reality? Happily, in this alternative story I am telling, the adult world gives us five characters whose names all begin with C. The strange thing, though, in this land ruled by adults, is that the truth of these giants would not be so obvious to us, were it not for the arrival of the alternative, God the Child, on the scene. It is this 'young' figure, though not a new one, who helps us to see the power of these five giants, exposing their hold over us and opening up the possibility of their subversion.

First, there is *Chronos* or, to use his full name, 'Chronology', the giant who establishes the sequence, perhaps the passing, of time. The point is, according to this powerful giant in our landscape, surely only an Adult God can make any sense of God's relationship with time. After all, we call God 'the Ancient One', so it would be ridiculous to regard the divine nature as child-like. But there is a knot within the logic of Chronos, something that needs unpicking – because Chronos makes two simultaneous arguments about God: on the one hand, that God is 'outside' time, so any such human notions about the divine nature can only ever be metaphorical, pictures that creatively bring together reflections and distortions of the reality. It is, of course, a helpful way of answering the question of God's 'age', because a God 'outside' of time neither was ever young nor is ever ageing. If the giant Chronos is right, that while everything else moves through time God never does (except in the incarnational episode, though even then it is said without limiting divine nature), what this shows us is that 'adult' notions are no more sensible than 'child' ones; each and every one can be a pointer towards divine characteristics, but none can say it all.

But I wonder, again and again, what a child in the midst of this land makes of the idea of anything being outside of time? It is an act of imagination, appealing in that sense, but its meaning is necessarily elusive. What does an engaged God, concerned with our predicaments, really mean for us, if 'outside' time? For our current purposes, though, the problem is also that Chronos regards God as being outside of time, while on the other hand simultaneously taking for granted that God is an Adult. But as an adult, does this mean God *was* young and has matured; or has God *always* been an adult? Of course, even if God is 'within' time, but has always been more like an adult, we should not imagine that adults are static; adults age too! In fact, even a God who 'ages', through billions of years, could still be 'young', in divine terms – since, it is said, a thousand years are like a day to God!

My point, though, is simply this: Chronos, the giant of time, tells us that it is logical either to see God as 'outside' of time, or that, if God is within time, God must be adult-like. But this giant is speculating and imposing its speculations on us, perhaps in accordance with the assumptions of powerful adults pulling his strings. It strikes me that if we believe Chronos assumes that God is both outside time and perpetually adult-like, it is no more absurd to regard God as being 'inside' time *and* perpetually childlike.[15] If divine timelessness is only an act of imagination, and God is actually 'inside' time, or bound up with time, this still does not mean that 'adultness' is the only sensible framework within which to conceive of God. Adultness makes no more sense than childness, not because of the question of God's 'age', which is something to which no human answer makes sense; rather, it is a matter of character – the childlikeness of

God – and the possibility of God's *perpetual* childlikeness. Arguably, God's 'maturing' through time could even be a deepening of divine childlikeness. Such notions themselves are, of course, acts of imagination, speculations, expressions of play, but they are no more ridiculous than the adult alternatives and, in fact, arguably more resonant with a number of key aspects of divine character, which we will consider through the book.

The second giant resisting God the Child is the giant of *Communication*. How, after all, could a Divine Child communicate so articulately with us? It is because of the depth and beauty of divine self-revelation, witnessed in holy scripture, that we must regard God as Adult. Surely. And yet there are a couple of key assumptions at play in this assertion: first, that children cannot articulate profoundly, which is very dubious; and second, that divine self-revelation is actually articulate and clear, which is also open to question. In fact, a model of God as Child could help to make a good deal of sense of the struggle experienced by humans in trying to pinpoint what God is saying to us. Many of us would say that even where scripture seems unambiguous, this does not automatically mean that 'God' spoke clearly, as such; rather, humans are deeply involved in the process, not only of interpreting the revelations, but in the writing and editing of them. What we have, in our holy texts, are the results of divine/human entanglements, wrestling with questions and experiences, sometimes expressed as clearly as the passionate appeal of a justice-seeking child, or a piercing scream of an infant, weeping or giggling hysterically, other times more like burbles or a child's emerging efforts to make a point.[16] The giant of Communication can be humbled by the honest wrestling with divine self-revelation; perhaps, after all, the divine life need not be so adult. Perhaps God can be, in part, inarticulate.[17] I come back to this in Chapter 6, in relation to the Bible.

But third, surely the giant of *Creation* establishes the adult credentials of God? We want our God to be *our* creator, not *our* creation. We must do all we can to ensure that God is the originator, and an Adult God helps to reinforce this. If God is Adult, this maintains the proper sequence: God created; it was not God's children who created God. As such, God the Adult, the parent of all creation, is the Alpha. In contrast, God the Child runs too close to the terrifying possibility that God is our offspring, the product of our own imaginations, something that must be resisted.

This giant, however, is not as sure-footed as we imagine. For one, why would an Adult God make it any less likely that we have played a real part in 'creating' what we believe to be true about it? Adults project things on to other adults, just as children do. Our minds are active in interpreting *and creating* the world we live in. We are creatures of imagination, so an Adult God does not insulate us from the possibility, in fact the likelihood, that our notion of 'God' is partly a construction; the mind being 'a perpetual factory of idols'.[18] Of course, 'God' *is* partly a construction! This is the point about religion's concern with idolatry: a healthy awareness that we always run the risk of creating God in our own image, and bow down to the thing we create; so we should perpetually interrogate our assumptions, to see whether we have settled for something too fixed, too 'set in stone', too taken-for-granted. An Adult God.

While the notion of God as Adult may help us to feel that God is the grown-up here, who created us as children of God, the reality is that God as Child creates a more honest conversation, in which we recognize the perpetual danger of our and God's co-creation. For we make one another, and we make God too. It will never be possible for us to draw a neat line between the very truth of God and the additions or distortions that we attribute to God; but what we can do is recognize such a reality and be active in our self-interrogation, our collective interrogations, of what we think and how we live. The possibility of God the Child exposes the delusions at work in our theologies, how God is 'our Child' while also our originator. In any case, children are creative! They construct whole new worlds – but they also tear them down and start again. In Proverbs 8, there is even a beautiful ambiguity in the Hebrew, that where God's Wisdom is described as a master worker it may also be a little child; for children can indeed be ingenious architects and builders. God the Child therefore stands as a challenge to the giant of Creation, who imagines we can avoid the issue of our involvement in 'creating' God; God the Child instead reminds us that we are active in this process – and that our models can change. In fact, if we are to change the world, to make it more like God's new world, maybe our God-models should be re-created too.

The fourth giant is *Completeness*, an issue I wrote about in *Holy Anarchy*. The thing is, adults can be a little anxious about the notion of God the Child, because it makes God seem 'incomplete', a God who is 'not yet' whatever it is that God should be. This too betrays some assumptions: first, that we imagine adults are 'complete', whereas most of us recognize that adults, like children, have fragilities; there are parts of ourselves that seem 'unfinished'; we are works-in-progress, until we die. In fact, in becoming adult, we have 'lost' part of ourselves in some respects. We gain, but we also lose, throughout our lives. This is why adults sometimes distinctly affirm the need to 'recover' childlikeness – in terms of playfulness, imagination, wonder. It is about the recognition that adults are *different* from children, but not more complete. We are all, in fact, complete and incomplete in different ways; we 'are', and we 'become', simultaneously. Second, then, the notion that an Adult God is 'complete' is just as problematic as that a Child God is 'incomplete'. There may even be a case for saying that a child is more fully themselves, not yet having learned the conditioning that the world instils in us; more free of the lenses and assumptions that gradually take root within us; more alert to the possibility of different realities. Perhaps.

But it is also worth acknowledging, as process theology does, that if God is within time, the notion of divine incompleteness may be on to something important: that God is genuinely open to the changes that happen, that they affect God, so God is on a journey of growth, in a sense not yet being the God that could be. This does not mean, if this God is 'Child', that God will become 'Adult', as though the journey towards completeness is only ever about the metaphor of ageing; rather, as I indicated above, God's maturing may be a deepening of childlikeness. (Also, of course, the different metaphors of God's nature are not mutually exclusive; God can be child and adult simultaneously, just as God can be male and female and non-binary. Each of these is an act of imagination, which may nevertheless catch hold of an element of the reality.) I return to 'in/completeness' in Chapter 7.

Finally, the fifth giant is the one called *Control*, in many ways the most powerful, as its name suggests. It is an obstacle to the possibility of God the Child, but exposed by such an image because it regards the Adult God as being necessarily in control of things, the whole landscape, the content of religion and what possibilities there may be at large. If God is in control, God must be Adult, surely? But once again there are assumptions at play: first, that a child cannot also exercise dynamics of control, as though adults have never known children's capacity to see their will done; the sheer power of an infant to beckon us and bend us to their will. But second and more importantly, it is the notion of control that is itself problematic. In a world of giants, the desire for divine control – and therefore an Adult God – is as much about a yearning for order, a certain sort of order, holding at bay the forces of chaos, and therefore a yearning for something like the status quo, which is at work here. The idea that God is in control can feel reassuring; that pattern can be found in the mess, that a deeper plan underpins the random-ness, that injustice can be put into a different perspective – it is the Adult God who helps us to see the parameters and obey accordingly. In contrast, God the Child enables two things: an alertness to the falsehood of such prevailing 'order', because the patterns and plans of the world seem so often to deny God's justice and defy God's lifegiving desires; and the opening up of space in which we dream of alternatives, like a child in pursuit of a new world. The notion of Control, this impressive, oppres-sive giant, is exposed as ungodly; the possibility of liberation and renewal emerges; and it is God the Child who sparks this adventure.

Each of these giants – each in some way a construction of human adults – is exposed and humbled because of the sub-versive power of God the Child. Chronos, Communication, Creation, Completeness and Control are all seen for what they are: human desires to maintain things a certain way, failing to wrestle with the ambiguities of life and religion, and the struggle for something different.

Of course, if we take the lead from Roald Dahl's story *The BFG*, we could conclude that each of these oppressive giants can be succeeded by the Big Friendly Giant instead. We could maintain God's adultness, while focusing on different versions of it, or the ambiguities and assumptions that I have explored here. But, actually, as friendly as the Big Friendly Giant is, it is the child in the story – Sophie or Wisdom – whose power is vital and transformative. It is the child who makes it possible for the giants to fall.

Are we nearly there yet?

This book, then, is an exploration of the childness of God, not simply as a speculative adventure in the mysteries of divine life, but to draw certain challenges and possibilities to our attention. It is shaped around three key themes – smallness, weakness and curiosity – that together subvert the giants we have been naming.

One question recurs, though, at least according to a range of conversations in which I have first aired God the Child: am I 'idealizing' childhood, by associating it too closely with God? I find this a very interesting question. My mischievous response is to pose another question: Doesn't the presumption of God as Adult very much 'idealize' adulthood? After all, when people express concern about God as Child, they refer to children's selfishness or lack of thought – which of course should make us think about the far greater evils of adult bad behaviour. In other words, the issue is not really that I am 'idealizing' childhood, by focusing only on the good traits of childhood, but that I am making selections, as though we don't continually, and perfectly appropriately, make selections when we seek human ways of characterizing God (the Adult). That said, within the three broad themes, my selections of childhood characteristics, idealized as they may be, are not characteristics that everyone would emphasize: in particular, the spirit of disruptiveness, even chaos, that I suggest is intertwined with God as Child and may not be everyone's idea of an ideal. The point is: we make selections whatever metaphors we work with, and God the Child helps to illuminate that this always occurs, not least when we take God the Adult for granted. In presenting the angel/God-figure as a child, the 2014 film *Exodus: Gods and Kings* made quite different selections, as discussed by Richard Walsh: for the child concerned is a 'petulant child deity', a 'brat – with terrifying power' who evokes the question in Pharaoh, 'What kind of fanatics worship a killer of children?', and is perhaps a sign of Freud's 'uncanny', our 'repressed infantile complexes'.[19] By contrast, my selections seek to call such power into question.

Essentially, my intention is to acknowledge that I am being selective and that, as an initial attempt to outline the implications of God the Child, this is inevitably – and indeed always would be – incomplete. It is not systematic, but in a sense more poetic; it has rough edges, not neat and tidy conclusions; it is an exploration in the subversion of God the Adult as much as it is an argument for God the Child, not to dismiss the adultness of God but to add to it, complexify it and reorientate us towards a different priority. To that end, we certainly are not 'nearly there yet'.

In terms of the selectivity, I focus on three interweaving themes. Each is outlined in a little more detail at the beginning of Parts 1, 2 and 3. Here I note that Part 1 is concerned with the 'smallness' of God, in the light of the classic notion of God's omnipresence. I wonder whether God can be everywhere but always small like a child. This is focused on the smallness of a child's hand, receptive to reality but not controlling it; which leads to a re-framing of God's 'grace' as 'solidarity' and, in engagement with Black theology, affirms that divine *location* is committed to change.

Part 2 explores the 'weakness' of God, in contrast to the classic concept of omnipotence, suggesting that God's power consists in 'chaos', re-framing God's action for justice in the context of playfulness and, through dialogue with Disability theology, suggesting that divine agency builds solidarity through coalitions of mutuality.

Part 3 turns to the question of 'curiosity', different from the traditional picture of omniscience. This is expressed in terms of the image of 'horizon-seeker', re-framing faith as imagination, and acknowledging the queerness of this quest in particular dimensions.

In the Conclusion, I attempt to outline the limitations of what I am doing and the areas for potential development. I draw the strands together by way of a 'God the Child creed' that offers possibilities for the church and the world.

Questions

1 Why do you think our images of God tend to be adult?
2 What do you think the problems are with the image of God as Child – and what is its potential?
3 What do you make of the problems with the five 'giants' supporting the Adult God?
   i *Chronos* claims that God is outside time but also an Adult – really?
   ii *Communication* claims that God must be adult to communicate with us – really?
   iii *Creation* claims that only God as Adult keeps us from playing a role in creating God – really?
   iv *Completeness* claims that God must be adult, because a child is incomplete – really?
   v *Control* claims that God must be an adult to maintain control – but is God in control?

Notes

1 Adrian Thatcher, 2006, 'Theology and Children: Towards a Theology of Childhood', *Transformation*, 23(4), October, pp. 194–9, especially 196–7: 'God the Child represents all children before God'.
2 Janet Pais, 1991, *Suffer the Children: A Theology of Liberation by a Victim of Child Abuse*, Mahwah, NJ: Paulist Press, pp. 14–16, 23.

3 See R. L. Stollar, 2015, 'God Is Child: The Child-Centric Christ-ology of Janet Pais', 7 December, https://rlstollar.com/2015/12/07/god-is-child-the-child-centric-christology-of-janet-pais/?amp=1 (accessed 13.9.23).

4 Pais, *Suffer the Children*, p. 87.

5 Pais, *Suffer the Children*, pp. 83–4.

6 Pais, *Suffer the Children*, p. 61.

7 Pais, *Suffer the Children*, pp. 1, 15; capitalization in original.

8 Stollar, 'God Is Child'.

9 R. L. Stollar, 2017, 'Jesus as Child', *Patheos*, 14 June, https://www.patheos.com/blogs/unfundamentalistparenting/2017/06/jesus-as-child/ (accessed 17.11.23).

10 R. L. Stollar, 2023, *The Kingdom of Children: A Liberation Theology*, Grand Rapids, MI: Eerdmans.

11 Wanda Deifelt, 2021, 'The God-Child Paradigm and Paradoxes of the Incarnation', in Marcia J. Bunge (ed.), *Child Theology: Diverse Methods and Global Perspectives*, Maryknoll, NY: Orbis, p. 74.

12 Deifelt, 'God-Child Paradigm', p. 76.

13 Deifelt, 'God-Child Paradigm', p. 84.

14 Graham Adams, 2022, *Holy Anarchy: Dismantling Domination, Embodying Community, Loving Strangeness*, London: SCM Press, pp. 110–11, 115, 165, 225.

15 See also John Hull, 1985, *What Prevents Christian Adults from Learning?*, London: SCM Press, p. 224: he suggests God 'is both the ancient of days and the eternal child'; and, p. 225, that God may be the 'perfect experiencer of time', for 'to experience time is to take time seriously'.

16 For instance, Janet Pais, in *Suffer the Children* (p. 59), refers to Jesus' cry to Abba as 'babbling', 'a childish cry'.

17 Adams, *Holy Anarchy*, p. 137.

18 J. Herman Bavinck, 1966, *The Church Between Temple and Mosque*, Grand Rapids, MI: Eerdmans, p. 122.

19 Richard Walsh, 2018, '"What Child Is This?": Reflections on the Child Deity and Generic Lineage of Exodus: Gods and Kings', in Richard Walsh (ed.), *T&T Clark Companion to the Bible and Film*, London: T&T Clark, pp. 311–21.

PART I

Wherever God is, God is Small

How big is God? Without always naming it, there are prevailing ideas around the size of God, on a number of fronts: first, in light of our growing appreciation of the scale of the universe, God has to be at least as big, because God is surely everywhere, in touch with every atom, every fraction of dark matter, every galaxy and black hole as well as the whole of this particular planet. So God has to be seriously big, if not bigger.

If we go round the world ten times, that is about the same distance between Earth and its moon. The moon is held there by Earth's gravity. Gravity is a relatively weak force. The Sun has gravity, and holds us in its orbit, though we are roughly 380 times further away from it than the moon is from us. The Sun is big (864,000 miles in diameter), but not by stars' standards – many are a hundred times bigger, and in fact there is one, UY Scuti, which could include five billion of ours. The next nearest star is four light years away – which means it takes light four years to reach us. Light travels fast. Quicker than that. So this star is a long way away, and it's just the nearest. Not quite as quick, a few Google searches tell me further cosmic factoids: in our galaxy, there are between 100 and 400 billion stars. There are 200 billion galaxies, or thereabouts. The universe includes about 70 septillion stars – that is, 7 followed by 23 zeros, which is approximately 10,000 stars for every grain of sand on Earth (I didn't count them all). Most galaxies are between 3,000 and 300,000 light years in diameter. In case you didn't know, the universe is big. Possibly not infinite, but not far from it! Such a universe surely demands an even bigger God, since God must be in touch with every particle, and anti-particle, of it.

Second, there is a felt need for the sheer grandeur of God, a majesty that cannot be contained, an inescapable impossibility, defiant in the face of the reductive reason of any culture; a God whose size and power are greater than anything else; a God who commands our devotion, even while dealing mercifully with our failures. That is to say, God's grandeur, whether poetic or soulful or holy, has to be on terms beyond our comprehension. God's majesty demands scale. Third, in light of the smallness of our vision, our containment of God within particular religious propositions, loyalties and boundaries, there is a recognition that God overflows the limits of our thinking and behaviour, defiant in the face of our own over-confidence. That is to say, however 'this' tradition conceives of God, we must remember with due humility that God is 'more than' our conceptions, our creeds, our commitments. Our hubris requires God's greater-than-ness.

So how does the lens of 'God the Child' review such assertions? This is not to deny divine omnipresence – that God is in touch with every detail of the vast universe – but it is to offer a child-sized vision of the nature of that presence. To stoop to see it differently. A scale that is simultaneously both vast and miniscule. A wonder bearing all things, all questions, challenges and gifts, but somehow in fragility; so wisp-like, so under-the-radar, so unnoticed, that it is almost not there: like a tiny hand, outstretched, open, but overlooked.

Beginning in Chapter 1, I consider the smallness of God, specifically in terms of the image of the open palm, a child's palm, focusing on its receptivity, its tenderness, its subversion of traditional parental dynamics, and its potential 'uncleanness'. In Chapter 2, this is developed in light of the theological theme of grace, divine receptivity as solidarity in the midst of all things, not least in contexts of fragility, despair and unbearable loss; an image of the child's non-innocence amid a traumatized world. Finally, in Chapter 3, if this has within it the potential to be 'universal' at all – that is, an image that can transcend cultural limitations – this is only possible if it is also decolonizing; so I seek to unpick the colonizing tendencies of the Great Big God through exploring the Blackness of the hand, how engagement with particular experiences of marginalization is the way to deeper solidarity.

I

God the Open Palm

'Whoever welcomes one such child in my name
welcomes me, and whoever welcomes me welcomes
not me but the one who sent me.'
(Mark 9.37)

Imagining

Dear God,

I've been thinking.

I hope you don't mind if I tell you what I've been thinking about, but I guess you're good at listening, like a really big ear.

Maybe some time you can tell me what you think about my ideas – I'm sure you know where I live.

Anyway, the recent pictures from the James Webb telescope have amazed me, so I've been learning a bit about the size of things.

Did you know, there are about 200 billion galaxies in the known universe? Well, that's the universe as it's known to us. I suppose you might know differently.

In the Milky Way, which is the galaxy where I live, there are at least 400 billion stars – and even our star, which we call the Sun, is over 90 million miles away, so imagine how far away some of the others are! No, further than that!

In fact, the distance across our galaxy is about 105,000 light years – a light year is how far light travels in a year, which is a long, long way, because light travels *really* fast. Much quicker than my friend who always wins the races at my school Sports Day.

Anyway, they say that our galaxy is part of a supercluster of galaxies, which is about 500,000 light years across.[1]

So, if you get the picture, things are really big.

This made me think about you, because it makes sense for you to be really big too.

If you're as big as all of those galaxies, it's amazing that you are interested in this tiny little bit of things, here on Earth, and it's amazing that you know my name, and you even know my favourite colour. (It's red, just in case you needed to check.)

But I've been thinking.

What if you're not as big as everyone says you are? I mean, big things can be a bit scary. I suppose when you see things that upset you, like people hurting other people, maybe you would get a bit scary. But most of the time, I don't think you're scary. In fact, I'm not even sure that you're a grown-up, not *literally*.

No. I think you're small.[2]

Sure, you're everywhere, in every corner of the universe, but wherever you are, you're always small. That's how I think of you.

Like something in the crack in our front wall, or hiding on a comet, or inside someone's tear when they've been hurt, or in a seed in the soil.

You know how babies have really tiny hands, which stretch out, and sometimes close and open again. They look so ready for everything.

I think that's a bit like you.

Like an open palm.

You're ready for everything, sensitive to more and more of your universe. So small that we can't quite see you, and we forget you're there, but still you're keen to be in touch with all of it.

There's something about the open palm that makes me stop and think.

Of course, sometimes you grip on to things, with all your strength, like a baby clutching on to someone's finger – and sometimes you hold on to us, really tightly, and nothing we do can loosen your grip.

But more often it's the open palm that grabs my attention, ready to receive, or to experience, or simply to be.

And that's you, showing that you love us by letting us bring everything that we have to your open hand, or by being ready for whatever the universe throws at you.

You never shut us out.

You never turn us away.

You never close yourself off from us or the 200 billion galaxies.

Your hand is always open.

Anyway, that's what I've been thinking.

Sure, you may be big enough to be in all of those galaxies, but you're also small enough to be in every photon, every little crack, every hidden corner, every place or experience or feeling that the rest of us may not notice.

You're there, hidden away, but always open, like a tiny little hand.

Ready.

So that's what I think.

If it's not true, never mind – though don't be too abrupt when you say so. Instead, maybe you'll help me discover for myself.

Thanks for listening.

Open, fragile and adventurous

Of course, an open palm in itself does not necessarily mean God is 'small', and of course an open palm is a metaphor: no more or less definitive than the wise old man, the midwife, heavenly radiance, the righteous judge, the ultimate shepherd. But as I also hinted in *Holy Anarchy*, I want to ask what happens to our God-modelling if we pursue this image as the primary way of seeing the divine life.

Rather than the parental figure, the personality of a child's open palm conjures up something a little different; not necessarily in conflict with the One who parents us, since the hand also offers an image of bearing our lives, as though holding, nurturing, releasing us. But it is primarily the receptivity of the hand that matters here (a theme also discussed in Chapter 6): the divine readiness to receive all of life, whatever is thrown at it, the bad with the good, without controlling it; an expansive sensitivity, never closed or shut off, transcending every tribe and class and perspective – but at the same time it is a *child's* hand, expansive yet fragile, or small enough not to grasp whatever it reaches out for, but still present, eager, yearning, stretching.

We are conditioned to imagine that God the Adult extends to us, has the sheer scale and magnitude to reach out to us, embrace us, hold us, bear us; that it is the Adult God who holds us on their chest, comforts us, listens to our cries, settles us – and none of this need be wrong, but it must not be the whole story, because God the Child comes to us with their tears, their sensitivity, alert to when we are upset, in tune with our heartache, clambering close to our tired bodies, simply *being*.

This fragility can unsettle us. We read in scripture about the dangers of being 'children, tossed to and fro by the waves and carried about by every wind of doctrine, by human cunning, by craftiness' (Ephesians 4.14), susceptible to the overbearing power and manipulation of others. If this understandably concerns us about humanity, prompting us to safeguard the well-being of children, to protect them from such abuse of power, then might we also need to safeguard God if God is childlike? And, in fact, arguably this is what we see – people's desire to protect God, to preserve God from all the things we might do to distort the truth of God. Accusations of blasphemy and heresy are attempts to keep God safe. But, of course, these desires are not at all shaped by any notion of divine childlikeness, as though the defenders of this model actually believe God is vulnerable and needs protection. Instead, these desires emerge out of our own sense of fragility and insecurity, claiming and enforcing boundaries in order to protect ourselves. Elsewhere, I have discussed the notion of 'heresy' and how childlikeness may speak into those arguments.[3] Essentially, following the work of Andrew Shanks,[4] the root of the word 'heresy' may be not so much about believing the 'wrong' things, but more about misguided intentions to cut people off from one another – the Greek word, *hairesis*, being related to dissecting, or cutting off. That is, heresy is the effort to restrict relationship and close down conversation, since such unneighbourliness is the negation of the gospel. If so, then childlikeness – at its best – arguably represents the alternative: the imaginative possibility of ongoing relationship, the risk or adventure of pursuing new horizons, free from adult obsessions with boundaries and divisions that keep us at bay from one another. After all, it is adults who are the heretics: when they impose walls and condition one another to be separate, suspicious, fearful; whereas children can point towards a better way, energetically breaking through the cracks in the walls, asking the awkward questions, dreaming big and boldly taking leaps.

So a childlike God does not need protection, but space to be boldly adventurous; even as humans (especially adults) tend to focus instead on the correctness of one answer or another, the appropriateness of one judgement or another, the grammar of faith and its detail, purporting to preserve the authority of God (or scripture) but actually desiring their own security in a world they know to be insecure. A childlike God can't wait to break free from these reins and run towards the next playful possibility.

But of course it is precisely this kind of childlikeness, defiant and apparently deviant, testing the boundaries and daring to presume 'It does not have to be this way', that unsettles adults, even frightens them – and makes us concerned that no one should be 'tossed about' like children. After all, adventurers go astray and get lost. This is why young children need play pens, so they don't hurt themselves. It is for their own protection. For their own good. And this is about human fragility, not God's. This insistence on the fragility of childhood surely means God cannot be childlike at all. God must not be vulnerable. (Except perhaps on the cross ... to which we will return in Chapter 2.) Instead, we're effectively told that God must be the one who constructs the limits of our playpens, so that *we* are not tossed about or hurt. And this gives *us* – or rather, certain representatives among us – the right to continue that work of keeping vulnerable people within limits for their own good. *For our own good.*

The danger emerges into the light: our theological anxieties cause us to yearn for certainties in a world of ambiguity and risk, and to require that other people work within the parameters that we find necessary. Churches have perpetuated this, again and again. They are often churches that grow numerically, at least for a period, because an uncertain world engenders a longing for boundaries and people who seem to have definitive answers can be attractive – but often some people discover a need to push against these very boundaries and answers, in the light of life-experience, and churches do not always know how to handle this. Meanwhile, others never seek out such theological security, instead finding meaning in approaches and communities where the thresholds are much lower, apparently fuzzier, but generally more accepting, giving more room for wondering – and wandering. There is freedom to question, doubt, explore, re-imagine. Attempts to control or delimit, even when portrayed as protection, are seen in a new light. Such churches, with blurred boundaries, may command less fervour and often struggle to grow numerically, affirming a different sort of growth – but even the question of growth, of course, is riddled with dilemmas and questions. Perhaps the very quest for security, stature, success or growth is not the primary way in which God is present with us. Perhaps there is something in the childlikeness, the smallness, the insecurity.

The reality is that, even as adults, we are also always partly childlike. This is nothing to be anxious or ashamed about but rather something to be embraced: the susceptibility to new learning, changing minds, discovery, imagination, renewal – these are signs of a living faith, attentive to a dynamic world. And it is arguable that such sensitivity and dynamism does not only go to the heart of who we are as human beings, God's *children*, but goes to the heart of God: the primordial Child – an attentive, learning and discovering God, in a perpetual state of re-encountering a dynamic universe, adventuring with it, even 'tossed about' by it, in fragility and vulnerability, riding the waves of change, open to new futures. (I return to this in Part 3.)

As I suggested in *Holy Anarchy*, the idea of two kinds of truth can help to illuminate this dynamism: on the one hand, 'truth-in-hand', which is the assertion of and claim to possess a truth with a degree of closure, maintaining particular, identifiable values, knowing one's identity and offering it with confidence to others. God is partly like this, but the problem with humanity is that we often give priority to this kind of truth, within ourselves and in our conceiving of God, so closing ourselves down to reconfiguration, and closing God down to the possibility of dynamism. On the other hand, 'truth-in-process' involves a disposition towards truth that recognizes that what we hold cannot be the whole story; there is always more; there are other layers and angles and connections; in fact, the lines we make when trying to identify the truth of things are more importantly lines of (partial) connection than lines of (definitive) separation; so we grow empathetically in our appreciation of one another's strangeness, insights, pain, and potential, and solidarity grows. We seek to peak behind the curtains where the wizard is manipulating the levers of power and control. We take the red pill to see the reality of the Matrix in the 1999 film of that name. Like eager and inquisitive children, we ask probing questions, again and again, seeing through the bluster of the first or second answers, which are designed to close the conversation down. God is more like this than truth-in-hand, since God's love, or grace, or neighbourliness is a disposition towards ever more experience, ever more diverse situations, ever-new futures.

This spirit of openness is more childlike than adult-like in tone and texture; it is God the Child, conceived of in terms of the truth-in-hand of deep neighbourliness, an ever-open palm extended towards a messy and dynamic universe, which is fragile in its adventurous prioritizing of truth-in-process: the glorious susceptibility to all that the cosmos may throw at it.

Small but not parochial

But of course the image of God the Child, and especially the child's open palm, is not simply an assertion of divine openness or sensitivity; it is also a provocative declaration of divine downsizing. How, if God is genuinely omnipresent, can God be so small?

The thing is, though, that an adult need not be everywhere either. Just because we conceive of God as Adult, that in itself does not say anything about God's presence in every part of the universe. It is more a claim to divine age, and authority, than size. But the adultness of the divine does also help us envisage scale: a God big enough to be everywhere, whereas God the Child conjures up a sense of smallness – and how on earth, or how in the heavens, can God be small? What sort of God is that?

However, conversely it is possible to insist that God the Child can still be vast. The notions of adult/child that we are exploring are suspiciously human, in any case, so if we allow ourselves to be set free from such human-centredness, of course a child God can be everywhere – it is a child *God*, after all. *But I specifically want to talk of divine smallness.* It is, vitally, metaphorical – it 'is' the case and 'is not' the case simultaneously, playing creatively with our sense of size and scale, but seeing the divine life through the lens of childness, stooping to do so, bending low to revisit what otherwise we might take for granted, is intentionally subversive, to draw our attention to a particular paradox, as I noted above: God is everywhere, but wherever God is, God is small.

Not an overbearing presence. Not an imposing body at all. But a breeze, a wisp, a whisper, a butterfly, rather than a hurricane or a yell, or an imposition. God is small. Barely making a footprint, barely breaking a twig, barely there, but simultaneously everywhere.

God is small. Small enough to be in the spaces that we neglect. The spaces we forget. The cracks. The hollows. The hideaways. Where broken toys are lost. Where the little can squeeze, either for some sense of safety or because the giants have backed them into a corner. God is small enough to be in the margins, places of shame that are vast yet overlooked, or sites of new beginnings, ridiculous in their insignificance, but from where surprises and transformations emerge or burst, or resurrect.

The thing is, we are conditioned to think negatively about smallness, in some respects – because it seems parochial, incapable of expressing the breadth and depth of connection that we would certainly expect of God. Even when churches celebrate smallness, as in an infant baptism, it is quickly connected with the mystery of the universal church – it is as though this child's smallness does not matter, because they have become joined, in Christ, to something huge, a global family that crosses the bounds of time. Or, in communion, we celebrate the smallness of the bread and the sip of wine, not intrinsically as smallness, but as capable of representing or embodying the vastness of God's love. After all, only things of scale, across time and space, can truly reflect the reconciling purpose and power of the divine. Parochialism, by contrast, is a problem; it suggests disconnection, separation from that which is other, other neighbours and enemies and experiences; it is unable to witness to God's barrier-breaking dynamic. And smallness seems to equate to parochialism, whereas God needs to be big.

But I do not think that smallness needs to mean parochial. On the one hand, the parochial in itself is not always a problem, because it is about being attentive to the local – being authentically present to a certain time and place in all its intricacies and nuances; so if smallness means this, all very well. But if the parochial is also about being cut off from otherness, because a parochial mindset presumes that what we have 'in here' is sufficient and the very truth of things, then smallness can indeed challenge this. Smallness, by virtue of being in the cracks, in the overlooked places, in the sites of possibility, can in fact express the deepest attentiveness to situations, beyond any parochial (or closed) mindset. Greatness, on the other hand, can be too focused on the big picture to notice the hidden stories. Smallness can be better suited to hearing, seeing, attending, where greatness may be too aloof.

Another way of putting it is to say that God the Child, by virtue of their smallness, is *pre*-tribal, *pre*-parochial: in the moments and spaces where things *have not yet become parochial*. As we grow, sometimes we are eager to tidy up the stories that we encounter, to make experiences fit into things as we see them, to gather together the common ground and people of like-mindedness, because it is a messy world, and we need ways of managing it and organizing it, and feeling safe within it. We may also, perhaps occasionally, work to overcome such boundaries, recognizing their limitations and the dangers of such inward-facing confidence-building. But it is God the Child, small enough not to be gathered up into adult patterns, who witnesses to an alternative: deep attentiveness to what is overlooked, solidarity with those in the margins, making possible what our adult insecurities impede – that is, a new sense of connectedness, defying parochialism.

In fact, I would suggest that an infant baptism represents this alternative, precisely because it is also a celebration of God the Child, their love for and solidarity with little ones, present with each of us even before any parochial forces take hold of us. It is not an immersion into a separated community, a family defined by blood, as such, but is an immersion into a possibility – a pre-tribal dream of connection with all and any who are little, belittled, overlooked, least and last; it is, in fact, an extended family defined by water, not by blood. Of course, it is related to – inseparable from – the particular story and community, and blood, of Jesus, his ministry, death and resurrection, and the body of believers who seek to follow his way; and in that sense, a distinct parochial project, local and global, with an identity of its own. But if we think in terms of the truth-in-hand of the immersion, baptizing us into a specific story, community and tradition, then the greater truth of it, its truth-in-process, is that each child is immersed into the pre-tribal, anti-sectarian, boundary-crossing vision in which all the little places are reconnected with one another, all the forgotten stories are reconciled, all the sites of injustice are transformed, all the giants are humbled, the least and last come first – all because of, or rooted in, the smallness of God the Child.

So too in communion: the smallness of the gift of bread and wine is intrinsically valuable, not simply as a cipher of something grander, but as a symbol of the value of smallness. A death in a rubbish-dump, Golgotha, outside the city walls, memorialized and held by each small hand in communion, is not a vast event – a battlefield strewn with bodies, across time and space; but is a deeply local event, a marginal event in a vast empire; it is a demonstration of solidarity with the small places, the overlooked cracks in our world, and – through the disconcertingly local event of resurrection too – the smallness of new beginnings, under the radar of the empire, is enacted. It is this very smallness, this very attentiveness to what is generally overlooked or belittled, that we hold, taste, ingest through the mystery of communion. Here we greet, or are greeted by, God the Child: small enough to give value to every instance of brokenness and every site of re-creation, in their very unnoticed-ness.

Attending to pain

It is important to appreciate that this vision of God the Child is not a romanticizing of childlikeness, as though this renewed focus on divine attentiveness suggests that childlikeness is always attentive. After all, children can also be both as single-minded and as distracted as adults – either staying too focused and ignoring peripheral realities, or losing focus, drawn away from what is in front of them, meandering or wandering or wondering elsewhere.

But two things. First, distractedness is not an issue per se, because it can sometimes be right to be distracted from the things that normally preoccupy us. The adult world often wants us to stay focused on certain things, giving less attention to stories that could be more important – for example, the media keeps us focused on many things that are relatively trivial while failing to ask other sorts of question about the structures we take for granted. In that case, distraction can be a process with the potential to reconnect us with reality. Even being distracted in daydreaming should not simply be dismissed as a waste of time, because it is a necessary part of processing our realities, helping us be in touch with imaginative possibilities, breaking free from the world we assume to be inevitable and glimpsing flashes of something different. In other words, attentiveness and distractedness are not opposites, because they interact.

Also, even though single-mindedness may take us away from attending to the breadth of reality, it is not necessarily always such an issue, because it can be profoundly creative. New possibilities for transformation often only occur when people give such single-minded attention to a particular problem. Children lose themselves in play, or in creativity, and this is important – it hones skills, concentrates the mind, enables learning and development.[5]

If the attentiveness of God the Child (attentive to all the forgotten places and the sites of possibility) seems to romanticize childhood, the point is more to affirm the significance of giving due attention to reality and its nuances and potential. It is simply that the childness of God expresses this attentiveness incisively through the *smallness* of God's presence, in the cracks and hidden places.

Second, though, this focus on attentiveness – the capacity of the child's open palm to be receptive to all of reality – is precisely *not* a romanticizing, because it is focused on the stories of the little ones. Not only children, but all who are rendered little in a world controlled by giants, bullies and systems. God the Child's openness to these realities, in a way that God the Adult can sometimes fail to express, is very much about being alert to the pain of the world.

Of course, our traditional picture of God as Adult is indeed said to be loving towards all, attentive to all, in a way that humans struggle to be. I do not deny that this is how the divine should be perceived. But the problem is that the adultness of God can, in fact, be used as a shield, protecting us from the depths of reality's pain; an adult in control of things, supposedly, can insulate us from certain others' stories, by framing them through the lens of divine agency. That is to say, a focus on God as Adult who is in control of everything can prevent us from listening to the reality of people's stories. It is, ironically, a romanticizing of adulthood that is the issue: as though an Adult God is in control of these things, the size and scale of the Divine representing their authority over such questions, and re-presenting people's lived experience *as though it somehow witnesses to a God of control.* Even where this Adult expresses vulnerability, as on the cross, it is said to be an enactment of God's plan.

It is such adult theology – that is, theology focused on the adultness of God – that represents the barriers of the playpen, purporting to keep us safe from our insecurities by telling a story to explain hardship. It is a soothing story, dressing up the harshness of the world in neatness. Meanwhile, theology focused on the childness of God dares to represent the end of adult theology, its insecurity-complex and over-confidence, and instead breaks out of the playpen by telling a quite different story about divine agency, one that is somewhat more 'out of control'.

Regarding this divine agency, as I noted in the introductory section, it is not only adults who create. Creativity goes very much to the heart of childlikeness – creativity that destroys and rebuilds, as in the spirit of Jeremiah, called to pull down and overthrow, pull apart and uproot, build and plant (Jeremiah 1). But as I shall develop further, in the next chapter and more in Part 2, the agency of this God as Child is not the same sort of agency seen in the controlling work of God as Adult; it is a different story, a different narrative, a different explanation. Its focus is not in giving an account of hardship, as though to tidy up our experiences of pain and trauma, but in attentiveness to such things, as in an open palm alert to each hidden instance of suffering. This can be no romanticizing. It is instead a reckoning with the trauma often borne by children, inflicted by an adult world; the traumas that God the Child bears, crying inarticulately but incisively in response.[6]

Furthermore, this hand, this open hand, this hand attentive to pain, is necessarily grubby. It is not a clean hand, but bears the dirt of the earth, the blood and tears, the scratches and cuts, the bruises and burdens. An unclean hand, at one with those rendered unclean by an adult world. Bearing shame. Bearing rejection. Bearing the cost of marginalization, silencing, sacrificing. At the same time, though, it is in the places, the small places, from where new life bursts forth. Digging into the earth, turning the soil, nudging at the stones, like an earthworm quietly, blindly, at work, aerating new possibilities.

God the Child, like an open palm, should not be under-estimated. It does not have the power of an adult, as we shall see, but it is nevertheless a force to be reckoned with. Fragile, susceptible to the struggles of life, attentive to them in ways that cannot be fully grasped, in the little places, in solidarity with little ones, and in sites of possibility. Never overbearing, never imposing, but nonetheless at work, unromantically; subverting the insecurities of the adult world, breaching the playpens of our adult theologies, witnessing to a pre-parochial vision of solidarity among all-comers, all forgotten and belittled, in which we are being immersed.

Baptizing with God the Child

We come to celebrate life – not simply life itself, but small life.

Life that begins when it is hidden.

Life that thrives through the cord of connection between one creature and another.

In fact, a network of connections, where we who are animals depend on trees, which depend on the atmosphere and the water cycle, which need to be nurtured by we who are animals.

We celebrate life – a small life and a connected life – a life within a web of relationships. A web of creation.

In all these dimensions, both vast and hidden, wounded and wonderful, God the Child is alive.

Giggling with joy, crying in pain, connecting with us through eye contact, reaching for us with an open hand.

God the Child, fragile, open, adventurous, embracing life, greets us and shows us the intrinsic value of small life, small connections, every connection.

So we come to celebrate life – small life – graced by the God who was there first, as a Child, giggling with joy, calling life into being and into relationship.

And this water is sign of the waters of life, which were there from the beginning, the deep out of which life grew, and it is sign of the baptismal waters that Jesus, who embodied God the Child, entered and embraced.

And with this water, we immerse this life – this small life – in the possibility and celebration of deeper connection:

Cleansing and refreshing, upholding and blessing, like a child in the womb, nurtured and nourished, and enabled and released to become alive with breath, with new connections, with wonder and love.

So as community, sign of wider connections throughout creation, attentive to the joys and the pain of life, we gather and baptize this life, this child, this gift, this treasure, immersing them in love that they may know fullness of life and radiate it.

Hymn: God, your hands are always open

God, your hands are always open,
ready to receive our all,
for your love is unselective,
not constrained by any wall;
love whose truth is still unfolding
through encounter with our pain
and our joys and all potential
shaping how you love again.

Yet your open hands cause friction
by revealing how we're closed,
or at least we're torn between them –
fists constricting, palms exposed;
hearts and hands incline to tighten,
so suspicions take control,
when we claim our grasp as certain
and demean the stranger's soul.

In the face of such division
where injustice breeds and thrives,
open hands become a judgement,
make us wonder what survives.

Threatened by your love unbounded,
'Crucify!' is our response –
but the tomb cannot contain you:
love won't end, not even once.

Though our faith proclaims this story,
still we're prone to tame its scope,
calming down insurgent loving
which can seem such foolish hope.
Yet your heart and hands remind us
love slips through the grip of fear;
and you trust we can pursue it
till the open future's here!

(Graham Adams, 2023)
Suggested tune: *Abbot's Leigh*

Questions

1 What stands out for you in these ponderings so far?
2 What of God as 'open palm' – open, even vulnerable, to the entirety of life; learning and growing through such deepening experience; a God not in need of protection, but who embraces whatever the universe throws at them?
3 What of God as small – small enough to be in the cracks, attentive to what otherwise might be overlooked, present in solidarity with all little ones?
4 What of God as alert to pain – sensitive, empathetic, and also creative, making possible the tearing down of structures that hurt and the rebuilding of what brings fullness of life?

Notes

1 See Michael Welker, 2021, 'The Power of Engaging Theologies of Creation and Childhood', in Marcia J. Bunge (ed.), *Child Theology: Diverse Methods and Global Perspectives*, Maryknoll, NY: Orbis. Welker engages with children's interest in the dynamics of creation.

2 Joyce Ann Mercer, 2005, *Welcoming Children: A Practical Theology of Childhood*, Des Peres, MO: Chalice Press, p. 6. Mercer sees a focus on childhood as a way of doing theology, which is about 'starting small'.

3 Graham Adams, 2016, 'Doubting Empire: Growing as Faithful Children', in Vuyani Vellem, Patricia Sheerattan-Bisnauth and Philip Peacock (eds), *Bible and Theology from the Underside of Empire*, Johannesburg: SUN MeDIA MeTRO, p. 88.

4 Andrew Shanks, 2014, *A Neo-Hegelian Theology: The God of Greatest Hospitality*, Aldershot: Ashgate, pp. 13f.

5 David Hay and Rebecca Nye, 2006, *Spirit of the Child*, rev. edn, London and Philadelphia: Jessica Kingsley Publishers, pp. 73–4.

6 See Benjamin Perry, 2023, *Cry Baby: Why Our Tears Matter*, Abergavenny: Broadleaf Books. Perry argues that God does indeed cry.

Grace as Solidarity

*Then they came to Capernaum; and when he was in the
house, he asked them, 'What were you arguing about on
the way?' But they were silent, for on the way they had
argued with one another who was the greatest. He sat
down, called the twelve, and said to them, 'Whoever wants
to be first must be last of all and servant of all.' Then he
took a little child and put it among them; and taking it in
his arms, he said to them, 'Whoever welcomes one such
child in my name welcomes me, and whoever welcomes
me welcomes not me but the one who sent me.'*
(Mark 9.33–37)

A child and their Imaginary (Adult) Friend

Child:
I wonder. God is like this amazing open hand, a bit like my hand,
but more 'Goddy'. An open hand that's open to everything.
Ready for anything. But also small enough to be wherever
people feel really small. In touch with everyone's pain. The universe's pain. All that's broken. At the same time, it's in touch
with the tiniest tiny places where new things begin. In an atom,
but smaller. What do you think?

Imaginary Friend:
OK, I can see that it makes me ask some questions about God
as Adult. But I'm not sure yet how it connects with some of the
big ideas in our faith: like grace. What does it say about God's
grace?

Child:
I think I was just talking about grace, but not using the word. What if it's not just this big, humongous love that God pours out? What if it's also love that's small enough to be alongside everyone? Like how I can squeeze through the gaps in a crowd. It means I can be holding your hand before you know it.

Imaginary Friend:
You're saying that God's love, on the one hand, is like a huge pile of treasure, big enough for everyone. But what that means is that I have nothing to give that can compare. It overshadows me. Its generosity is everything. So, on the other hand, it also needs to be small enough to be alongside me, and to receive me, with whatever I have to give. It doesn't demand from me, like a bully. But it inspires me to give who I am, to find you standing there, in the cracks in the crowd. Your eyes gazing up. Noticing me.

Child:
Yes, that's it! And both of those things are childlike love. Big and bold, full of enthusiasm. But also quiet, humble, in alongside you, waiting to hear all the stories of the universe.

Imaginary Friend:
I see that. Children are always a mix of different things – just like adults! *You* certainly are. Sometimes precocious, exhaustingly vivacious, with unbounding life. Sometimes more reserved, shy, unassuming. Talkative or attentive. Rushing in or holding back. And you're saying God's love, God's grace, holds these together.

Child:
I think so. Big enough to be more than enough. Small enough to understand every experience of smallness, and to let other people's experiences find room for themselves. God's grace, love for all creation, is like a child's open hand: open to all of the universe, but child-sized.

Imaginary Friend:
I wonder if it's a bit like this too. It's like God being ready
for connection, no matter who we are, however deserving or
undeserving, small or grand, ready or unready; God's love
is energetically ready for us. Especially God the Child: seeing through us, to whatever we hide, all those stories, all the
treasures and the emptiness, making it possible for us to give
who we are because we see that we are accepted and loved by
God the Child. Small, open arms disarm us, give us time and
space to find ourselves. Like being invited to play a game, even
if we join in awkwardly, until we learn to be at ease with our
awkwardness, delighting in the Child's delight. Is this what 'the
reconciliation of all things' looks like (Colossians 1.20)? It's
like the power of an open hand, which seems empty, but which
invites us to become who we are called to be, which we grow
into – not upwards like adults, but downwards instead, redis-
covering our childlikeness, made in the image of God the Child.

Child:
Yes, you're on a roll! And what if God's grace is only like
a treasure, not because it's a big pile of grown-up love, but
because it's small – even fragile? After all, Jesus didn't seem
to think big things were all that important – wealth or status,
temples or kings.

Imaginary Friend:
Yes! Big things end up having too much control over us, and
control confuses us – it's not clear what holds our attention. It's
as though, when strength and majesty and power have a hold
over us, we think these things are God. But God the Child isn't
like that at all – not about control. But about risk.

Child:
I like this dream! True love is about risk. A childlike hand
reaching out, not knowing what will happen next. Not full of
riches, which could distract and confuse us; not promising a
huge amount of something to fix all our problems, but instead
a Child who is ready for us, just wanting to play, to hear what-

ever stories we have, to be present with us. Not controlling, but making connections freely.

Imaginary Friend:
But I've got a question for us. Are we suggesting that other versions of grace can be controlling? After all, children can also be controlling – even if they learn it from adults – but they need things from their carers, and they must instinctively evoke a response, if they are to survive. So a small hand can also be manipulative.

Child:
Good point. Let's go backwards to start with. First, this picture of God the Child is like poetry. Or art. It's not trying to answer everything – but it is trying to add to other pictures, because they're not complete. Without it, we could forget things that are in our memory, but which God the Child brings into focus. But second, it's also meant to stop us in our tracks. After all, adult ways of thinking can be so ridiculous! Like we can define God! Like we can grasp the mystery! Trying to say just the right things and expect everyone to agree. So God the Adult is sometimes a lot of hot air. We need God the Child to poke a bit of fun. I know the idea of God the Child can also be precocious – is that the right word? Sometimes thinking we've got things just right. But we need God the Child, to stop us saying too much.

Imaginary Friend:
And third, we're trying to be a bit playful – which isn't frivolous, but a serious business.[1] If all our thinking about God involved grown-up logic, we would soon find ourselves deep in absurdity, so there has to be room for poetry and play. (More of this in Part 2.)

Child:
Back to your question: how other versions of grace can be controlling.

Imaginary Friend:
I'm wondering, perhaps this is the problem: when people insist that God's grace is a vast store of treasure while we are seen as empty. This allows them to argue that God does everything, and everyone simply has to receive it just as they're told.

Child:
Yes, people – especially adults – claim that it's as simple as that, but actually what they're saying is that people should think what they think. The 'God' who does it all, and shares his vast treasure, is a bit like a human giant in disguise, telling people that they are weak – and keeping things the same.

Imaginary Friend:
Of course, it is good news that God's love is big enough to be for everyone – in fact, for all of the universe. But at the same time, who controls the story?

Child:
God the Child doesn't! It's not a story about control. But about how God relates to space – not filling it, but small enough to receive whatever is happening in the very smallest spaces. In touch with the pain, the questions, the curiosity, the anger, the confusion, the play, the dreaming, the poetry.

Imaginary Friend:
A God who's small enough to take us by surprise, especially when we're being too adult. A God who doesn't control the story, but risks whatever is thrown at them, the many stories of life and struggle. A God who especially embraces the stories that haven't been heard because they felt too small.

Child:
Yes, a God glimpsed like an open palm, alert and ready for anything, especially for whoever might be overlooked, sparking their story to be heard as they come out of the shadows. This is grace, the building-block of true community; not treasuring size and strength, not thinking of us as empty or keeping us silent,

but stirring us to become whoever we are, at our own pace, to arise and delight in the open hand of love.

Imaginary Friend:
I like that – and you've said it better than me.

Child:
We did it together – like we always do.

Suffering and solidarity

So far, I have alluded to something that needs much more direct engagement: the question of suffering. I have been suggesting that the model of God as Child can help us to see various issues differently, not that it should replace all other models, but should stand alongside them, and disrupt them. How, then, does this model enable a different approach to suffering?

Before we get into any detail, I must acknowledge two things: first, that it is certainly not possible to say that this model will 'resolve' the issues. Of course, if I was offering it simply because I thought it might be 'helpful', I am aware that critics could say it is merely a contrivance, a projection of human desire, a reconstruction of God in light of our expectations of how God *ought* to be, to serve our particular aspirations. This response would be unfair, because exactly the same critique can be made of Strong Man theologies, or indeed Adult theologies in general, which can also be regarded as contrivances, or projections of *some* people's desires – and a significant part of my own argument is that God as Child helps to expose the way in which Adult theologies *presume* so much, not least in terms of an apparent 'need' for a God 'in control'. These theologies are inseparable from the status and power held by adults in the real world, so they arise from somewhere in particular, speak to somewhere in particular, and leave little room for alternative possibilities. I accept that people will judge 'God the Child' similarly.

But the thing is, 'God the Child' is not only about trying to be helpful, as though 'designed' to meet particular needs. After all, not everyone will find it helpful, even if they are drawn to models of divine weakness, because God's childlikeness still does not 'resolve' the issue of suffering, certainly not where suffering is so abject, horrific or inexplicable. The first caution here is for myself: I must remain aware that, even if I feel that God as Child may speak helpfully into all sorts of difficult situations, it is not an 'answer'. Theorizing and theologizing can help to make sense of experience, arising from the rawness of life and death, and I believe that God as Child can be seen in those terms, but that doesn't make it an all-encompassing framework within which everything and everyone finds the answer. Silence, instead, does a better job of taking suffering seriously. We will come to this shortly, in engagement with Karen O'Donnell's profound work about pregnancy loss.

Second, as I have begun to hint there, this model of God the Child brings us up against very difficult issues and situations. Of course, God as Adult does so too, but there may be a particular sensitivity when childness is the backdrop for the discussion or the lens through which experiences are viewed. It is important to note this, because I must be aware, in my thinking and writing, that I may be stumbling into territory with a degree of clumsiness or awkwardness, unintentionally but nevertheless with repercussions. It is a second caution for myself, but also for the reader. If my writing does indeed stumble into experiences without due regard for all the layers of emotion, my apologies in advance for not accounting for these sensitivities adequately. My hope, though, is that by naming examples of particular kinds of suffering, we may see what this means for the possibility of God the Child.

In addition, it is important to note how this model evokes attentiveness to difficult situations, because this stands in contrast to an 'adult' presumption of children's 'innocence'. Of course, we adults should seek to protect children from anguish in all kinds of situation, preserving their right to grow safely as children, rather than bearing the weight of adulthood before their time. (We should do this, and we seek to do this in many respects, even while also participating in an economy that exploits children, sexualizes them and turns them into economic agents themselves – so our desire to maintain their innocence is itself compromised by our behaviours.)[2] However, we tend to do something more than *aspiring* to preserve their innocence: we want to believe that they *do* live in a state of innocence, even though another part of us knows that they are more alert to the traumas of life than we care to admit. Within the home, the community, the wider world, children 'sit on the stairs' (metaphorically or in actuality), overhearing their adult carers, alert to the conflicts of life in all its shades and colours. More than that, they directly suffer because of adult behaviour: war, domestic violence, hunger, neglect, abuse and much more. Far from being a romanticization of God, the model of God as Child locates God's presence in the midst of all kinds of suffering, even under the radar of adult attention, even where we do not care to look, where we do not admit the reality, where we pretend things are otherwise.

God the Child, then, plays this twin role in relation to suffering – attending to it in ways that confront us with its reality, while also risking such exposure to multiple kinds of pain and trauma that the discussion may stir up distress in us. So be gentle with yourselves when reading this. Difficult questions will be raised, and things will not be resolved.

At the heart of this discussion is the question of divine suffering or, more directly, what it means to think in terms of divine *solidarity in the midst* of suffering. This, after all, is the nature of the open palm, the childlike open palm; that its attentiveness to every overlooked experience is about solidarity in the midst of suffering, whether hidden or public. My argument is broadly that God is the ultimate empath, one who is especially sensitive to others' pain. But this needs to be explored in relation to questions of suffering – not only where childlikeness demonstrates such alertness, but where childness is at the centre of the suffering. This is why I will be engaging with the crucial work of Karen O'Donnell in particular – not that she addresses every possible instance, but she explicitly engages with pregnancy loss as a way of exploring the nature of God's involvement in suffering.

O'Donnell raises a caution about 'solidarity'.[3] In effect, she notes that solidarity can be asserted rather too hastily or clumsily, as though God's own suffering on the cross expresses divine solidarity with all of our pain, on the basis that such suffering shows us that God 'knows' what it is like for each of us to suffer. How, though, does crucifixion give God knowledge of, for example, pregnancy loss? It is certainly bizarre, if not offensive, that Christian theology often talks all too easily about how God's experience *in Christ* acts as giving God access to universal human experience – his incarnation gives him access to all human life, and his death gives him access to all human suffering. This is indeed problematic.[4] For me, it makes much more sense to argue that God's *omnipresence* – as 'small' as it may be, in terms of location in the midst of every overlooked corner and in the midst of every site of unlikely possibility – is a better basis for God's empathetic openness to our diverse experiences. In fact, if the former (Christ-centred) approach is seen as the basis of 'solidarity', then I agree with O'Donnell that it is hugely problematic. But I also add that I do not understand solidarity in terms of God sharing the 'same' experience with us in any case. Solidarity, at its best, should not rely on common or shared experience, but on commitment to relationship *even where such commonality is less obvious*. As we shall see in Chapter 6 too, Claire Williams also insists that solidarity holds 'sameness' together with 'difference', rather than supposing solidarity is only possible where there is sufficient commonality.[5] So divine solidarity does not require God to have the 'same' experience as others, but to be committed to relationship even where that same experience is lacking. This, after all, is what empathy entails: feeling others' pain, even where we have not experienced it ourselves.

Just to reiterate, though: this empathy, or solidarity, is not reliant on the cross, as though direct lines can be drawn from the crucifixion of Jesus to his empathy with all suffering. Rather, it is the omnipresence of the open palm, the hand of God the Child, which may act as a more vulnerable but reliable basis of such empathetic solidarity. I return to this very shortly. However, as regards the cross, there are of course different ways in which we could account for God's presence or suffering there. This is not the focus of my discussion, since I am rooting God's empathy in God's omnipresence – but I need to address the cross, because it raises particularly sensitive questions for the claim to God the Child.

There is the question of how God is present to the suffering in crucifixion – and the model of God the Child heightens the tension between two different approaches. After all, even though it is a critique that is itself criticized by mainstream theologies, many people express concern, if not outrage, that Jesus' death on the cross appears to result from the abusive will of his Father; it looks like Divine Child abuse, exacting on Jesus (the child) suffering that he does not deserve (indeed, no one can deserve it). The response from mainstream trinitarian theology is that such a distinction between the Father and the Son is not appropriate, because the crucifixion represents God's will to take the punishment for sin on to himself, the Father and Son being 'one'. Strikingly, though, in the context of pregnancy loss to which we return shortly, Serene Jones makes the poignant argument that, by virtue of the death of the Son, the Trinity holds within itself the experience of bleeding and child loss.[6] All the things that women bear in this experience, as explored by Jones's research, may also therefore be borne by God: a 'death of hope', 'a death that consumes God', as the 'borders' of God bleed, rendering God 'helpless' yet bearing the 'guilt'.[7] This 'anti-maternal narrative', as Jones describes it, enables God-who-miscarries, or who loses a child, to be 'with' women, if they can imagine it – but Jones also anticipates that this may open up space for 'new ways of relating' in which God's grace is not seen in images of mothering but in maternal loss.[8] Of course, as for all interpretations of the suffering on the cross, these possibilities must be handled sensitively – especially where there is any risk of excusing or valorizing suffering itself or even justifying violence.

The nature of God's suffering – whether held in an integrated Godhead (Father, Son and Spirit involved together), in anti-maternal narratives or in the Son in particular – is important here, but it is not the whole of the story. That is to say, it is only relatively recently that Christians envisaged *God* suffering. For most of our history, God was not understood as capable of suffering, but post-Shoah (post-Holocaust), specifically in Jürgen Moltmann's argument of *The Crucified God*,[9] it became more mainstream to see that God does suffer, in solidarity with us. The divine/human Jesus, an integrated whole, bears the actuality of suffering in his body *and* suffers in terms of the experience of God-forsakenness, the experience of God's apparent absence in which God's presence is real.

This still leaves us with huge questions, of course – questions that are heightened if we conceive of God as Child. For what are we to make of the suffering of the childness of the divine? It is a painful question. On the one hand, we could argue that it makes a difference whether or not this suffering is *God's will*. If it is God's will, even as God takes this suffering on within the divine life, what are we to make of God the Child willing such suffering? There are significant issues when Christians emphasize the divine will for suffering, because it has been used to justify – or at least excuse – other suffering. As I argued elsewhere, we risk affirming 'God of the crucifiers', a God on the side of powers and systems that do violence to others.[10] It might be preferable – and I think it is – to argue instead that the crucifixion of Jesus shows us God's solidarity with those who are subjected to abusive power. It is about God 'of the crucified'; in which case, the cross is not God's will but a sign of how God bears the pain inflicted on those in the margins, and indeed those who push against such systems. It is the will of the system, and God the Child bears it in solidarity with all little ones, all who are demeaned.[11]

But in either case, the assumption is still that God experiences suffering directly, and that this is somehow the basis of God's 'knowledge' of our suffering and of God's 'solidarity' with us. And in either case, there seems to me to be a difficulty in 'utilizing' the suffering of the Child, even as the Divine Child. Can a child's suffering bear any such utility – or meaning? Can a child's suffering be 'necessary' in order to give us something we 'need': an affinity between God and us?

I suggest something different, and that God as Child enables this imaginative alternative. God does not will the suffering of the cross. God does not will any suffering. In fact, God is the will for healing, comfort and justice, the soothing of pain, the overcoming of suffering. But God's will does not always come about – and how God's will may come about is discussed in Part 2. Rather than the cross being God's will, it is the imposition of suffering by a broken world, here on the person Jesus of Nazareth, who had repeatedly pushed against the systems of such a world, its cruelty, exclusions, injustices, inhumanity, indignities – and the world struck back against him, to silence him. His impulse had been a witnessing to the will of God the Child, who desires healing and justice for all. And in his death, we glimpse how the divine empath, one who experiences our pain through the imaginative capacity for empathy, the very basis of solidarity with us, is indeed with us – first in solidarity with Jesus, and in solidarity with us all, since Jesus bears witness to the universal scope of divine empathy, breaking barriers, transgressing boundaries, alert to every possible outsider.

There are difficulties in conflating God the Child with the Crucified God – dangers, in fact, since such a collapse between the two could encourage us to justify or excuse other suffering, especially suffering inflicted on little ones. Instead, God the Child highlights the danger: beware any tendency for adults (or human giants/powers-that-be) to do harm to little ones (actual little ones, or figurative little ones – those with relatively less power in the world). And the alternative is to emphasize the divine capacity for imaginative empathy – solidarity 'with' Jesus, and solidarity with any or all of us, not on the basis of 'shared' experience or knowledge, but on the basis of this commitment to relationship, underpinned by empathetic openness to others' suffering. The cross, then, is not the *means* by which divine solidarity is effected, but a heightened *instance* of its significance, an expression of God's with-ness, even where God seems absent, or un-with.[12]

God the Child, an empathetic open palm, does not will suffering, but is alert to it, wherever it is found, in hidden places and in public view. As Dorothee Sölle argued, we are, in effect, God's ears, hearing the cries;[13] our hands are God's nerve-endings, through which God is attentive to pain, *feeling* it in solidarity with us through a profound capacity to empathize, effecting tears within the divine. It is God as Child who makes this imaginative capability come alive, and who calls us to participate with God and one another in such solidarity-building sensitivity. The systems of the world would rather divide us, and there is a cost in pushing against them, as Jesus knew too well, but it is not the end – and such alertness to pain, such alertness to the multiplicity of human experiences, such receptive imagination, evoking the telling of such stories, whether in words or in silence, is the nature of grace.

The loss of God the Child?

What, though, when the Child is not simply present *to* suffering, or an exemplar of imaginative empathy in solidarity with others' suffering – but is at the centre of the suffering? This can either mean the child themselves suffers, or adults' suffering is rooted in experiences concerned with 'children', such as infertility, unwanted pregnancies, pregnancy loss, stillbirths, child loss or any grief centred in the 'loss' of particular expectations around children. All of these are different, so I will not be addressing them in their respective details, but together they highlight how 'childness' brings to mind a wide range of experiences of suffering that cannot be 'resolved'. Their trauma remains.

In the context of pregnancy loss – or 'death in utero'[14] – in particular, as O'Donnell outlines, churches are prone to all sorts of trite responses to these tragedies; prayers are offered unhelpfully, insensitively, without regard for the reality of the feelings; and 'God' is evoked as though all such suffering is in God's plan, in God's hands, in God's timing.[15] Of course, there are various theologies that push against such triteness and which do not encourage any sense of God 'willing' these things, but instead they seek out better understanding and expressions of solidarity.[16] O'Donnell notes how feminist theologies express divine power differently, not over and above, but in relation, gently and persuasively. Liberation approaches imply that God's providence is limited in the cause of maximum freedom among all God's people; in other words, God certainly does not cause suffering, but creates the possibility of its overcoming. Black theology rejects any excusing of suffering in the name of God; rather, God exercises power that others may have the freedom to be. In process theologies, God is not only gently active within creation but is changed by the dynamics of a changing world, always being love but unable to guarantee that the divine will is done. (O'Donnell suggests that 'if God is present in the face of suffering but unable to do anything about it, then there appears to be little point in praying.'[17] However, I do not think this is entirely fair to process theology: it is not that God cannot act, but cannot guarantee that God's actions generate the desired results; God's power is persuasive love, not coercive force. Such activity must therefore find responsive participation within creation, and slowly confront the asymmetric powers that resist God's will.) Finally, O'Donnell refers to Elizabeth Johnson's model: she draws from Thomas Aquinas, for whom creation participates in God, and relates this to evolutionary under-standings, accentuating the potential for God to act through 'chance';[18] that is to say, God's ways are not enacted through orderliness, but through randomness – which has some affinity with my approach in Holy Anarchy.[19] For me, it is the possibil-ity of 'chaos' – the potential of a quiet, small, even if also angry, action-for-healing-and-justice, to effect greater transformations – that can be traced in these approaches; chaos that allows for surprising eruptions within the natural order, but surprises that not often, or regularly, occur. I discuss this further in Part 2.

But O'Donnell's key point in this discussion is that many theologies try to tidy up the issues; to find solutions for the question of God's apparent inaction; to suggest Jesus' death expresses all necessary solidarity,[20] whereas, as Delores Williams argues, it is his life that better demonstrates solidarity with those who suffer;[21] and any turn to the resurrection is all too neat, a resolution that is uncalled-for, when people are in the midst of trauma (the Holy Saturday of despair and fragility).[22] Mere solidarity, however, is not enough; there must be mean-ingful action.[23] It is significant, though, that the experience of loss, as well as any potentially meaningful action in solidarity, is always framed in relationship with others;[24] it is never simply an individual reality, even while the experience itself is deeply personal. For example, in her research with women who had experienced reproductive loss, Serene Jones discovered that it can be felt to be 'failure': this reflects particular expectations as framed in a cultural context – specifically expectations of productivity in an economic culture that celebrates 'efficient production'.[25] For the women, they believe they have 'failed'.

Rather than seek out neat answers in such complex experiences, in terms of what or who God is, O'Donnell indicates that it is much more appropriate to focus on what cannot be said, the denunciation, the apophatic speaking – 'God is not ...'[26] This makes me cautious about offering a suggestion – both because I am located outside of these experiences, and the question of childness is obviously intrinsic to the suffering here. But might it be possible that God the Child, a 'smaller' God if you like, can resonate in part with this quest for *what cannot be said*; a God who is not overbearing, but fragile; present but uncontrolling; a God who desires but does not dictate; a God who cries but cannot coerce? There is, then, an affirmation of God's open-handedness, but a denunciation of God's control. As John Caputo argues, 'strong onto-theologies' – theologies that rely on and assert the 'being' of God – run the risk of being too closely aligned with religious power; whereas 'weak' theologies (to which I return in Part 2) are more adept at speaking into sites of apparent absence, the ambiguities and uncertainties of life and faith and pain; it is not that God 'is', but that God may 'become'.[27] Of course, God the Child does not at all resolve these questions, because a child cannot be regarded as a 'becoming' with no current 'being'. A child *is* 'being' in itself – mattering in itself, valuable in itself. Intrinsic worth, as child. But there is nevertheless *also* a sense of the child *becoming*, growing into being, in a way that holds the tension between what 'is' and what 'could be'. But there remains a profound problem here: where the suffering is defined by *loss*, specifically the loss of a pregnancy or a child, surely 'God the Child' reinforces the pain? In this tragedy, the question is not God's being or becoming, not God's presence or potential, but the *loss* of God.

The centring of this loss prompts O'Donnell to wrestle with hope and hopelessness; it is a centring in which complex factors intersect, such as class and 'race', affecting how the loss is framed socially for different people.[28] Within such complexities, theologies that focus on hope do not see how they can become so toxic.[29] Miguel De La Torre says it is especially people in privilege who cannot see the deadening power of hope, imposing itself on people whose experiences are more familiar with and defined by hopelessness. 'You can be sure that it will all be OK in the end' – this is such a dangerous dismissal of people's lived experience, with no room for despair.[30] In the face of such optimism, O'Donnell argues for 'disruptions of hope'.[31] For De La Torre, this isn't a universe with a moral arc bending to justice, which is a colonizer's narrative, but is an amoral universe – though one also in which particular people have power to shape the narratives or control the biblical interpretations, the theologies of prayer and so on.

Is it possible that God the Child can attend to these sensitivities, *because* of the Child's inarticulacy? God the Child does not impose meaning or story or an arc, but poses the questions, and more questions, and remains with them – 'remaining' being a significant theme for O'Donnell. The model of God *cannot* be perfect, because no model can be, and this one runs profound risks, especially the risk that it may highlight and even exacerbate pain unintentionally – but at the same time, its ambiguity, its capacity to speak silently into loss, offers an absence-that-remains, 'rupturing' providence.[32]

But I also note the power of her arguments that the *imago Dei* is 'performed' in the body of the miscarrying person;[33] that this is not simply something happening 'in' a body, but that it is also, as noted above, a relational experience. It is especially relational in terms of how the foetus and woman affect each other, shaping and reshaping their respective identities; so the 'loss' is not only of the pregnancy but of the 'identity-in-progress' of the woman.[34] For Jones, as the woman's 'future she imagines collapses', so 'her hope dies'.[35] Not only is her sense of time reconfigured (the lost future), but the sense of self is 'disoriented', 'ruptured', 'fragmented'; even a sense that 'death becomes her', her body as a grave.[36] In the midst of such experiences, to ask a further question seems potentially dangerous: but is it possible that the model of God the Child may interact constructively with these realities? For example, if the *Dei* whose *imago* is performed in the miscarrying person is the childness of the divine, what are the implications? Does it 'help' to envisage the God who is in solidarity with such trauma as child-shaped, and in solidarity with the experience of death 'becoming her'? I am not exactly sure; but, as I say, I am not suggesting that the purpose here is to design a model that will help universally. Rather, I am posing the question: Does a Divine Child and their inarticulate empathy with others' suffering speak (awkwardly) of solidarity in the midst? Or is an Adult God more reassuring, yet more 'distant' from the question? Again, I cannot say; these experiences are not mine.

Nevertheless, perhaps the childness of the Divine testifies to these truths: first, the inarticulacy, the piercing scream of an infant, the inability to make meaning out of life's shit, is well expressed by God the Child. Second, God's nature cannot be romanticized as though to paint a more beautiful picture out of such awfulness, and the childness of the Divine arguably helps to highlight the unresolvable pain. And third, the fact that God the Child poses uncomfortable questions in the face of child loss or pregnancy loss enables us to see how other models, associated with God the Adult, perpetuate their own insensitivities. For no model can do everything, but it may be 'preferable' for our models to illuminate the pain than to pretend no pain is caused – though who decides whether this is the case?

Returning to the relational dimension, not only is there the loss of a being, the foetus, but also the loss of an identity-in-a-state-of-becoming: the woman's anticipated movement from not-a-parent to parent, which is a subjectivity in relation to others.[37] I wonder, what are the implications of this loss of 'identity-in-progress' being an experience with which God the Child expresses solidarity, however inarticulately? The point here is that God the Child does not 'know' the woman's experience of such a loss; nor the experience of a man, or woman, whose partner has experienced a death in utero. After all, as

Jones discovered, it is 'a portrait of suffering that is painfully unique': 'a self without a future', one 'whose borders are as fluid as the blood she cannot staunch', who feels herself to be 'the anti-maternal self', even 'an imagined killer'.[38] As we saw above, Jones suggests that God *may* experience these, in the sense that, through a trinitarian understanding of God, we can conceive of God bearing within Godself the loss of the Son – an anti-maternal narrative. Even so, God does not 'know' what each woman's experience is, only God's own experience. God, whether Adult or Child, is not experiencing another person's suffering directly, but nevertheless feels it.

Perhaps, though, it is the childness of the Divine that helps to express this: the limits of one's experience, even God's, are real, because one never knows another's experience, not precisely, not even an experience apparently 'the same'. Divine solidarity, however, is not rooted in the commonality between God's experience and another's, but in the empathetic imagination, which is bound up with divine omnipresence. God, who is everywhere, though small enough to be 'in' everything, is attentive to everything, like a sensitive open-palm, but still does not 'know' exactly how others feel; rather, God's childlike capacity is to imagine it, as closely as possible, as deeply as possible, by envisaging and naming the distinctiveness of each anguish, bearing the story of each person in their relationships and context, and yearning for their good even in the midst of all the shit that they bear.

Such is grace, rooted in the childlikeness of the divine life.

Welcoming the Child

To draw this chapter to an 'end' (though not a resolution, but instead a holding together of the speculations offered here), I return to the biblical verses quoted at the beginning: that in the context of the disciples' argument about who is the greatest, Jesus placed a child in their midst, but also said that to welcome a child is to welcome both him and the one who sent him. That is to say, that in the presence of a child there is greatness and, in the coming of a Child, God comes. It is an episode richly explored, for instance, by Joyce Ann Mercer, for whom such welcome signals the significance of children as 'gift' and as fully human in themselves,[39] and by Corneliu Constantineanu, for whom the welcoming of a child calls forth the total reversal of social power and status.[40] I too explore it in a chapter about mission.[41]

Since, in these words, Jesus is emphasizing the deep connection between the presence and welcoming of a child and of God, this leaves open the converse truth: the painful possibility that, in the loss of a child, God too is lost. But should this be so? It need not follow automatically, though it is surely understandable that the two losses may feel inseparable. Or perhaps the truth of it is in the loss of certain *notions* of 'God'. This is something O'Donnell suggests: traumas have the capacity to prompt us to stop worshipping particular models of God.[42] In that light, and because of such awful possibilities, the expression of God's *presence*, or God's *being*, must be cautious, even necessarily ambiguous or weak. Otherwise, a supposedly emphatic statement of presence will try to do too much work, too much heavy lifting, in the face of terrible experiences where meaning or resolution cannot easily be found.[43] Instead, remaining (or perhaps abiding), and silence (or inarticulacy), and the restraint of any effort to make meaning, may be better signs of God's presence, in the midst of tragedy. It is not that God comes definitively in the coming of a child, or only by such means; nor is it that God is necessarily lost in the loss of a child; but the centring of 'the child' (human and/or divine) evokes particular sensibilities: the power of God's absence-that-remains, the smallness of what is great, the emptiness of what is abundant, the power of what is weak, the receptivity of what is gracious.

God's solidarity, which is God's grace, is therefore to be understood as empathetic solidarity: presence that understands what it does not know, imagination to feel others' pain even where there is not shared experience, attentiveness to what cannot be articulated. It is these child-shaped sensibilities that show us that God is (possibly) coming.

Hymn: Wrestling faith

In faith we wrestle with our God
who calls us all by name;
we find no easy answers come
and yet we're not the same:
our honest wrestling changes us –
we bear the joy and pain
which shape the people we've become
and how we'll change again.

In faith we plead with God in prayer
who calls us to persist,
but justice does not always come
as forces still resist:
so through our wrestling and our prayer
we bear the hope and cries
till forces change and freedom comes
and those bowed down arise.

In faith we glimpse the ways of God
who writes on hearts so frail –
the ways that do not strongly come
and do not just prevail:
they come, instead, like one who limps
in struggling for what's right:
so know that wrestling's part of faith
till daybreak ends the night.

(Graham Adams, 2022)
Suggested tune: *Kingsfold*
Based on Genesis 32; Luke 18; Jeremiah 31

Questions

1 What about God as the divine empath – not 'knowing' the experiences of our own pain, since they are not God's experiences, but capable of imagining and so feeling their truth, empathetically?

2 In situations of pain or trauma, how *may* it be helpful, or at least partly resonant, to conceive of God's *presence* in terms of weakness or inarticulacy?

3 How might these approaches, rooted in God *as Child*, represent a different way of thinking about God's grace: not as an abundance that fills empty people, but as an open hand, which lovingly receives the multiplicity of stories and experiences?

4 I suggest this model enables us to see grace as 'solidarity': attentive to our every struggle, question, experience, trauma, longing and potential, even though those are not God's direct experiences, and enabling us to build gracious/empathetic solidarity with one another – so that our agency matters and solidarity leads to action, even if it is inarticulate or silent. What do you make of this?

Notes

1 Brian Edgar, 2017, *The God who Plays: A Playful Approach to Theology and Spirituality*, Eugene, OR: Cascade Books, p. 1: 'play is of a higher order than seriousness', referring to Johan Huizinga, 1955, *Homo Ludens: A Study of the Play-Element in Culture*, Boston, MA: Beacon Press, pp. 211–12.

2 I discussed this in my chapter, 'Doubting Empire: Growing as Faithful Children', in Vuyani Vellem, Patricia Sheerattan-Bisnauth and Philip Peacock (eds), 2016, *Bible and Theology from the Underside of Empire*, SUN MeDIA MeTRO, p. 85. I discuss it further here in Chapter 5.

3 Karen O'Donnell, 2022, *The Dark Womb: Re-Conceiving Theology Through Reproductive Loss*, London: SCM Press, pp. 91f.

4 Rosemary Radford Ruether questions this assumption, back in 1983, in *Sexism and God-Talk*, London: SCM Press, pp. 98ff.; and James Cone questions it in, for example, 1997, *God of the Oppressed*, New York: Orbis, pp. 136–8: prevailing models coming out of particular experiences and therefore not being as 'universal' as imagined.

5 Claire Williams, 2023, *Peculiar Discipleship: An Autistic Liberation Theology*, London: SCM Press, pp. 107–8, 118–23.

6 Serene L. Jones, 2001, 'Hope Deferred: Theological Reflections on Reproductive Loss (Infertility, Miscarriage, Stillbirth)', *Modern Theology*, 17(2), pp. 227–45, 241–2, https://search-ebscohost-com.ezproxy2. commonawards.org/login.aspx?direct=true&db=rfh&AN=ATLA0001334757&site=ehost-live (accessed 29.7.23).

7 Jones, 'Hope Deferred', p. 242.

8 Jones, 'Hope Deferred', p. 243.

9 Jürgen Moltmann, 1974, *The Crucified God*, London: SCM Press, p. 243: 'the God who is dead and yet is not dead'; p. 280: 'divine *pathos*'; p. 283: 'the suffering of God'.

10 Graham Adams, 2022, *Holy Anarchy: Dismantling Domination, Embodying Community, Loving Strangeness*, London: SCM Press, p. 82.

11 In taking this approach, I am aligning myself with theologians like Walter Wink, for whom the cross is the act of the Domination System: God in Christ is subjected to it, exposes its moral bankruptcy, so undoes its authority, but still was not the agent who willed it. See Walter Wink, 1992, *Engaging the Powers*, Minneapolis, MN: Fortress Press, pp. 139f.: 'What killed Jesus was ... not anarchy, but the upholders of order.' James Alison, too, sees it as a sign of the scapegoat mechanism, exacted against God in Christ, who duly exposes and subverts it. See James Alison, 1997, *Living in the End Times: The Last Things Re-imagined*, London: SPCK, pp. 24, 27, 141. Generally speaking, liberating theologies would agree: feminist, Black, Queer and so on.

12 For those interested in the technical distinction here, this is an 'expressive christology', where the life of Jesus expresses what God is generally and always about and up to. It is not, then, a 'constitutive christology', the very means by which God enters into human history and constitutes the means by which things change direction. God, after all, is always in the business of changing the direction of history – and Jesus showed this to us.

13 Dorothee Sölle, 1978, *Death by Bread Alone: Texts and Reflections on Religious Experience*, Minneapolis, MN: Fortress Press.

14 O'Donnell discusses various terminology, identifying how 'blame' is implied in 'miscarriage', how 'pregnancy *loss*' does not do justice to it, like 'misplacing' something, and perpetuating a sense of 'fault', and suggests 'death in utero' says what it is more directly, but acknowledges it may not be used widely: *The Dark Womb*, pp. 68–72. The range of terms is also discussed in Jones, 'Hope Deferred', p. 229.

15 O'Donnell, *The Dark Womb*, p. 77 (regarding triteness), pp. 99–100, 105–6 (regarding problems with prayers).

16 O'Donnell, *The Dark Womb*, pp. 85–91.

17 O'Donnell, *The Dark Womb*, p. 89.

18 O'Donnell, *The Dark Womb*, pp. 89–91; Elizabeth Johnson, 1996, 'Does God Play Dice? Divine Providence and Chance', *Theological Studies*, 57(1), March, pp. 8–17; Thomas Aquinas, 1956, *Summa Contra Gentiles*, trans. Vernon Bourke, Garden City, NY: Doubleday, chapter 66.7.

19 Adams, *Holy Anarchy*, p. 109.

20 She specifically rejects the triumphalist interpretations of the cross, in *The Dark Womb*, p. 120.

21 O'Donnell, *The Dark Womb*, pp. 92–3, citing Delores S. Williams, 2013, *Sisters in the Wilderness: The Challenge of Womanist God-Talk*, 2nd edn, Maryknoll, NY: Orbis, p. 167.

22 O'Donnell, *The Dark Womb*, p. 94, referring to Shelly Rambo, 2010, *Spirit and Trauma: A Theology of Reimagining*, Louisville, KY: Westminster John Knox Press, pp. 6–7.

23 O'Donnell, *The Dark Womb*, p. 94.

24 Jones, 'Hope Deferred', p. 230.

25 Jones, 'Hope Deferred', p. 231.

26 O'Donnell, *The Dark Womb*, pp. 99–100, referencing Nicola Slee, 2001, 'Apophatic Faithing in Women's Spirituality', *British Journal of Theological Education*, 11(2), April, pp. 23–37, specifically p. 25, https://doi.org/10.1558/jate.v11i2.23 (accessed 07.12.23).

27 Adams, *Holy Anarchy*, p. 108.

28 Jones, 'Hope Deferred', p. 231.

29 O'Donnell, *The Dark Womb*, p. 114.

30 O'Donnell, *The Dark Womb*, pp. 115–16.

31 O'Donnell, *The Dark Womb*, p. 117.

32 O'Donnell, *The Dark Womb*, p. 105.

33 O'Donnell, *The Dark Womb*, p. 49.

34 O'Donnell, *The Dark Womb*, p. 68.

35 Jones, 'Hope Deferred', p. 234.

36 Jones, 'Hope Deferred', pp. 234–5.

37 O'Donnell, *The Dark Womb*, pp. 68, 72.

38 Jones, 'Hope Deferred', p. 236.

39 Joyce Ann Mercer, 2005, *Welcoming Children: A Practical Theology of Childhood*, Des Peres, MO: Chalice Press, pp. 44, 49–50: the receiving of children, as the little, is integral to the counter-narrative of God's reign in the midst of empire.

40 Corneliu Constantineanu, 2014, 'Welcome: Biblical and Theological Perspectives on Mission and Hospitality with a Child in the Midst', in Bill Prevette et al. (eds), *Theology, Mission and Child: Global Perspectives*, Oxford: Regnum, pp. 139–40, 146–7.

41 Graham Adams, 2024 (forthcoming), 'Mission in the Colonial Matrix of Adult Power: Child-Centredness as Way, Truth, Life!', in Benjamin Aldous, Harvey Kwiyani, Peniel Rajkumar and Victoria Turner (eds), *'Lived' Mission in 21st Century Britain: Ecumenical and Postcolonial Perspectives*, London: SCM Press.

42 O'Donnell, *The Dark Womb*, p. 78.

43 O'Donnell, *The Dark Womb*, p. 125. Refers to Karen Kilby's caution about meaning: the importance of staying with the meaninglessness in Karen Kilby, 2020, 'Negative Theology and Meaningless Suffering', *Modern Theology*, 36(1), pp. 92–104, https://doi.org/10.1111/moth.12577 (accessed 07.12.23). I found a similar need in a discussion where some were wanting to 'make sense' of awful things using a theological narrative, and even sought to push against a culture of 'nihilism', in which nothing has meaning; whereas it struck me that 'Christian nihilism' is an important perspective: impressing on us that our theological narrative may actually ask us to live uncomfortably but empathetically with the meaninglessness of certain kinds of suffering.

3

The Blackness of the Hand

*The nursing child shall play over the hole of the asp, and
the weaned child shall put its hand on the adder's den.*
(Isaiah 11.8)

What might God say?
(Warning: this may be precocious)

I see you.

I see what you're doing.

I see that, by affirming my childness, my childlikeness, my
child-shaped life and love, you are illuminating how 'adult'
images have a hold on people, and on their imaginations, and
even on their practice. 'Here's a mirror, even if it's a bit
cracked.'

I see that you are being playful, helping people to throw
the various juggling balls a little higher, to see what happens when some fall, while others are caught, how the game
changes. 'Welcome to the circus!'

I see that the invitation to embrace the open palm of my
grace, and the attentiveness of my solidarity in the very midst
with people's pain, even where I cannot articulate meaning, is
an attempt to celebrate the depth and breadth of uncontainable, inexpressible love, which gives voice to multiple stories,
not least those who are demeaned, and refuses to make things
tidy. 'Come to the feast where change is possible!'

But I wonder ... do you see the danger? On the one hand,
you are clearly committed to my capacity to extend love to
all people, all experiences, all worlds, even in every hidden
corner and crack. It is a universal story. But at the same time,
might it be possible that your sense of the Child comes out

of a particular culture, a particular context, even your own story?

Might you be trying to tell a story for everyone, but in an accent or idiom that is not everyone's?

Might you be inviting all to affirm God the Child, while the Child in question looks more like you than like the diversity of human life?

Does your story need some decolonizing?

What I might say

You are right. There is that danger. In fact, it is surely more than a danger. I am surely envisaging childness as I understand it, or as I know it, even as I aim to be more imaginatively empathetic – but I must keep learning, keep being challenged, keep revisiting my assumptions.

This is why we turn now to the question of what it might mean for the open palm to be Black.

I am White, so I am trying to become aware of my Whiteness and how it affects what I think, say and do, but I have not seen it all yet – and I recognize that seeking out Blackness is not the whole of the story, because there are many different backgrounds that need to be recognized, voiced and addressed. So this choice is selective; it is a political choice: I want to engage with the questions of Black theology to see how they interact with this child-shaped theology that I am imagining, and to see what it might begin to mean to decolonize my assumptions so far.

Of course, I hope that the turn to the Child is in itself a decolonial act, drawing attention to 'the colonial matrix of adult power'[1] that frames our theology. I will come to this further in Part 2, but at the heart of it I am trying to decolonize the Adult framework with its powerful giant-figure, who colonizes the consciousness of our divine and human worlds. What might it mean for us, in our theological imagination and practice, to stoop to the child's perspective, to re-frame the Divine as Child, in order to see ourselves differently too? This is a decolonial enterprise. However, it is a work in progress, not least because my re-envisioning of the Divine as Child surely is informed by my context, including my Whiteness: so how might the Blackness of the small God open things up differently?

Like various liberative theologies, Black theology seeks to address how human life is framed in a particular way: racialized, divided and how oppression runs through it – and part of its argument is also that God must be re-envisaged, breaking out of the captivity of God's implicit Whiteness, and seeing the Blackness of God, God's solidarity with those demeaned and dominated in racialized terms.[2]

Similarly, Disability theology seeks to address how human life is framed in a particular way: divided by 'abilities' and how oppression runs through it – and part of its argument is also that God must be re-envisaged, breaking out of the captivity of God's implicit Able-bodiedness, and seeing the Disabled God,[3] God's solidarity with those excluded because of bodily differences. (I consider this further in Chapter 6.)

Also, Queer theology seeks to address how human life is framed in a particular way: divided by sexualities and genders, and how oppression runs through it – and part of its argument is that God must be re-envisaged, breaking out of the captivity of God's implicit Straightness, and seeing the queerness of God,[4] God's solidarity with those marginalized and dehumanized because of sexual and gender diversities. (I consider this further in Chapter 9.)

So too Child theology seeks to address how human life is framed in a particular way: adults determining the narrative and its rules – but, curiously, Child theology does not seem to have much of a tradition of asking how this relates to the very being of God, God's (potential) childness. (I return to this further in Chapter 5.) As I noted in the introductory section, the focus of its efforts is on Jesus as the God-Child, on his (briefly) *becoming* Child, not on the perpetual childlikeness of the Divine that I am advocating.

I want to learn lessons from this: that Black theology highlights a tension that Child theology appears to overlook. The relationship between the universal story (for all people) and the particular experience (whether Black or Child) is held together in the life of God, but only because a choice is made, rather than assuming one model speaks for all.[5] The choice, as James Cone insists, is that God must be Black;[6] without that commitment, the universal story is not possible, because Whiteness fails to express solidarity with all – and God's Blackness is about solidarity. For Cone, 'The blackness of God means that God has made the oppressed condition, God's own condition.'[7] Whiteness, instead, deals 'in abstractions about the love of God, while allowing racism, colonialism and empire to flourish'.[8] Similarly, then, God the Adult fails to reflect the universal nature of the story, and we must choose the Child (not as a replacement for all other images, but rather prioritized to redress previous imbalances). This is why Ryan Stollar argues much more explicitly for 'Child *Liberation* Theology', rather than simply 'Child theology': because what is required is actually liberation of children from Adult theology and politics, a centring of children rather than regarding them as symbols for something else.[9] Rohan P. Gideon also sees intersectional alignments among the various liberationist movements, incorporating and centring children, working for 'cooperative social transformation' through such child-attentiveness and intergenerationality.[10]

Incidentally, it is because of the intersections between different liberative movements that the child does not always come first. We see this in the story of Jairus' daughter (Mark 5.22–43). Although Jesus is on a mission to heal her, he allows himself to be interrupted by a woman who has been bleeding for 12 years, giving priority to her in her lack of status and class, while the daughter of a synagogue leader has to wait – and dies as a result. His key ethic that he proclaims, 'The first shall be last and the last shall be first', has uncomfortable consequences. In the process, though, he calls the woman a 'daughter' of Abraham, not a patronizing condescension but an affirmation of her invaluable childness – and as Anne Richards argues, he then does not let anything stop him from healing the girl.[11] Through the intersection, the story demonstrates a solidarity of daughters. Crucially, though, in the spirit of liberative movements, John

Baxter-Brown reminds us that: 'Children are not just to be objects of our benevolence or charity, but according to Jesus, they are active subjects in the Kingdom – the very ones writing the scripts that lead us to life.'[12] For Baxter-Brown, this 'Upside-Down Kingdom' has several key features – it is the very content of the good news, is associated with healing, can be entered or received, can be near to people, is grown rather than built, and has a different value system than the surrounding regimes[13] – and children, critically, show us the way into it. Within the web of intersections, child-centred theologies play a vital role.

The God who is everywhere, though small enough to be in every space, like an open palm attentive to every cry of creation, is therefore Child and Black. I am conscious, incidentally, of the danger of 'conflating' Blackness and Childness, which was part of the project of White supremacy, claiming maturity over Black bodies. My point is not to say the two conditions, of Blackness and Childness, are the same, but that there is a synergy in their exposure and subversion of patterns of domination: they act as allies of each other, by virtue of the system that denigrated their realities. There is, though, the converse danger: as was identified in the case of Child Q in the UK, 'Black children are perceived as more mature – and culpable – than White peers', due to an 'adultification bias', in which White adults project preconceptions of less vulnerability on to Black children.[14] It is appropriate to be conscious of this complexity, but what we see is that both Whiteness and Adultness must be addressed, to dismantle preconceptions and power dynamics – through the agency and power of Blackness and Childness. As we shall see in Chapters 6 and 9 respectively, Disability and Queerness also engage in an exposure and dismantling of such presuppositions and power; they are part of the same story of confronting 'giants' and their vested interests with the gospel's liberation of alternative possibilities.

To assert God is Black and Child is, then, a dangerous assertion, like a hand reaching over an adder's den, daring to play a game dismissed by some as 'identity politics'. Daring to assert a particular identity as the basis of the story's renewal of all reality. Daring to be selective. Daring to be bitten.

But the issue is: we are always selective. The question is: In whose interests are we selective?

Just to be clear: the selection of Blackness, like Childness, is not to denigrate White people any more than it denigrates adults – but it is a judgement. It is, as Anthony Reddie states, 'comfortable, White, middle-class believers' who, in Cone's Black theological inversion, 'will feel the cold wind of exclusion and judgment'.[15] Despite the realization that White Christianity had fostered indifference to Black suffering,[16] the demand of Black theology is not a call to self-loathing, nor even self-denial as such, because instead White people must honestly reckon with the self, in the context of the colonial matrix, rather than deny it. It is a call to deeper self-reflection, repentance (*metanoia*: 'turning around') and reparation; that is, daring to ask ourselves the question: What might it take to do justice in the midst of the wrongs that have been done in the name of an implicitly White/ Adult God?[17] It is, for Cone, a call to become Black, which, as Reddie explains, was never fully developed by Cone[18] – but, through Cone's affirmation of Dietrich Bonhoeffer's costly commitments, to Black people and then to Jews, we can see that:

> for White people to be saved, they need to identify with and enter in the struggle for racial justice to the point where the cost for doing so is a demonstrable example of their commitment to follow Christ and to be in solidarity with God through their solidarity with Blackness.[19]

M. Motlhabi, Allan Boesak and O. J. Phakathi describe such a process as a 'purposeful, systematic re-evangelization and conscientization effort' – one in which Whites too are liberated.[20] Rachel Starr suggests it can be expressed in terms of the need for 'unbecoming'; that is, a process in which White people and institutions do not allow themselves to be distracted by the desire for 'answers', seeing instead the need for 'unknowing', 'constant vigilance and critique of White privilege and the systems of White domination', and recognizing that the cost of failures are 'borne by Black and Brown friends, colleagues and strangers'.[21] If we relate this discomfiting but vital process to

God who is *Child* as well as Black, then the call to 'become like children' (or for adults' unbecoming) takes on demanding but liberating significance for adults.

If the divine hand is my symbol of God's omnipresent small-ness, in the same way as Blackness represents the particular solidarity of God with the oppressed, together they signal God's commitment to subvert systems that belittle and oppress. This is an expression of God's open-handed grace, which has a pref-erential option or bias towards those who suffer at the hands of existing structural biases – the 'asymmetries of power' or the closed hands that dominate. In other words, it is because our world already *is* distorted, meeting the needs of a few more substantially than those of the many, that God's attentiveness is seemingly 'skewed' towards the hungry, the homeless, the poor, the marginalized, those who suffer prejudice, exclusion and indignities. Of course, many White people and adults are included in those groups, in various ways. This is the insight of 'intersectionality', identifying how one set of injustices does not tell the whole story; injustices interweave with one another. The result is that some suffer in compound ways, many suffer and benefit simultaneously in different respects, while others enjoy multiple kinds of privilege. Womanist theologies have incisively revealed these interconnections between racialized identity, gender and class, arguing instead for a 'politics of wholeness' because, essentially, there are no good 'masters', whether of ethnicity, gender or class.[22] In this way, assertions of Blackness, Disability, Queerness and Childness highlight how God's uni-versal love interacts with us, in the cause of deeper solidarity. As I noted, though, in the previous chapter, Karen O'Donnell is clear that solidarity alone is not enough if there is no accom-panying ethical action; this is why self-reflection must lead to new commitments.

How might this work its way out?

Disruptive Child

I am prone to idealize the disruptive child because both elements of that, coming together, represent something integral to my theological enterprise: 'disruptiveness' in the face of assumptions, clichés and systems of domination, and 'childness' as the means by which such disruptiveness is expressed in the face of God the Adult.

But a review article by Selina Stone and Fr Simon Cuff highlighted the issue for me: it is more costly for Black children to be disruptive.[23] As I understand it, the issue is that there will typically be harsher consequences for Black children, in national environments in which they are minorities, because their disruption is noticed more and it bears a different weight of history within racist structures and legacies. Systems have a typical 'gaze' directed at those 'expected' to be disruptive, because it is a role given to them by historically conditioned narratives, and the costs will be significant; in contrast, those not 'expected' to be disruptive may be regarded as making a simple mistake, which can be whitewashed.

This is a comparable point to one I made elsewhere, about my greater freedom to be anarchic as a White middle-class man with many interlocking privileges,[24] whereas, for example, women run the risk of suffering greater prejudice, labelling and disinvitations. I enjoy several luxuries enabling me to play the game even disruptively.

This does not mean that I retract the claim that God the Child is disruptive, because such disruptiveness is a necessary part of decolonizing our theology and practice. But the cost of disruption within the gospel story is seen in a new light. For instance, a Roman citizen may be forgiven certain indiscretions, but a rebel rabbi, running the risk of being seen as a new messianic leader, cannot be forgiven for such dissidence. There can be no leeway. Then, when the early church in his name finds itself with female leaders, pushing against cultural norms, and proposing that members' property should be shared for the sake of the poor, the system cannot tolerate such disruptiveness and orthodoxy must fall into line – so we see church hierarchies regressing into conservative modes. After all, risks are borne differently by different classes and genders, as well as according to racialized identities and age. The costs are variable, depending on who is being disruptive.

God the Child, whose Blackness is vital, bears with those who suffer such costs of disruption. God the Child expresses solidarity with them. God the Child empathetically imagines their pain, without articulating or imposing meaning – and through such reception of multiple stories, divine grace reveals to us the truth of reality, its distortions and its capacity for transformation, truths we do not want to see. Such bearing, such solidarity, such empathy, is not for God alone, but is called forth in how we seek to follow and witness to an alternative anti-kingdom – through becoming Black, becoming children.

This movement is a coalition of many stories, with many different participants, some with few privileges, some with many; some bearing fewer risks in speaking of solidarity, some knowing the cost of it every day. Cone warns that oppressors desire to be Christians and oppressors,[25] and urges us to see that some choices have to be made: Whose side are we on? Of course, some people can be oppressors in some situations but oppressed in others, or a complex mix, according to intersectional dynamics of class, 'race', gender, sexuality, disability and age. But to disrupt privilege is to encourage one another to examine who presumes to speak, narrate, determine and resolve, committing instead to uncomfortable learning.[26] Disruption, in fact, calls us to see what we do not want to see, to hear what we do not want to hear, to process what we do not want to process, in pursuit of a future that no longer safeguards the interests of the privileged but, out of the ruins of the current dis/order, makes possible a new creation. Al Barrett and Ruth Harley warn against the notion of 'holding the space', as though it can be done neutrally, since White people are prone to control it;[27] instead, the discomfort of having Whiteness exposed and dismantled – as the framework within which White people can take various privileges for granted – requires a decentring of self, a depriviléging; and something comparable is involved in adults reconfiguring dynamics of power in relation to children.

An image of this may be the child playing with the building bricks, leaving some scattered around for giants to stand on, barefoot, causing them to stumble, while the work of demolishing and rebuilding goes on. I was asked about this recently, the anxiety that people feel when the rules seem to be changing, the ground is even shifting, and there is no longer the same kind of 'authority' holding it all in place: it occurs to me that this is what can happen when children take ownership of the game, wrenching it from adults who teach us to play within their parameters, whereas with children the rules can evolve, a new story being told, even a new goal emerging.

The Divine Child who inspires this is not to be romanticized or whitewashed, as though disruption can be done entirely respectably, within parameters that the privileged may find acceptable, and as though there will be no cost. Remember the rich young ruler (Mark 10.17–22) who, when he asked Jesus how to 'inherit' eternal life, as though it is much like receiving a gift from those who went before us, Jesus urged him to give up his inheritance: 'sell what you own, and give the money to the poor'. So too there is a disruptive call for those of us whose inheritance of privilege – whether age-related or racialized or both and more – is considerable, to work through what it means to give it up.

But care must be taken when we speak of costs or sacrifices. Jung Mo Sung reminds us that the alternative horizon to which we are heading must have the upper hand over any particular programme (or game) that we develop to help us reach there, because the horizon is one where no one is sacrificed to a cause;[28] it is instead a world free from such 'using'. Therefore, our means of heading in that direction should also not sacrifice people, make some expendable in the service of a mission, overlook the costs especially if they are borne by particular groups, or disregard the pain of disruption. Rather, we seek to build a world where none is sacrificed, so the road towards it must be similarly empathetic, while still disruptive for those who hoard their privileges. But when the disruption causes discomfort, how do we manage that?

We should remember, of course, that the status quo already

inflicts discomfort; it exploits, uses, sacrifices and ignores many people. This is not God's will. God the Child, who dreams of something different, recognizes the pain that is, and urges us to be realistic about the cost of changing to what could be. It is the smallness of such a God, present even in situations where pain is overlooked, that helps to bring these issues into the light, attentive to them and attending to them with fragility and energy.

So what kind of world might we be pursuing together?

The Child who won't be King

The argument is this: God's grace is demonstrated by an open palm, a child-sized palm, small enough to be in touch with the smallest of places and sites of possibility, attentive to their every story, their pain; not articulating or imposing meaning, but in silent solidarity with any and all. And this solidarity is deepened because of the hand's Blackness, a symbol of its rootedness in the particular experience of those who suffer at the hands of skewed systems and vested interests. (Of course, it is not only about a hand, but the Child's small hand signifies that divine/human possibility, reaching out in longing.)

This entails a creative tension – which is not a phrase that fully captures the difficulty of what is involved here. It is an agonizing tension. On the one hand, there is the good news of the universal story of grace, which includes divine love for multiple enemies: even love for those who oppose such grace; even somehow love for those who overlook the fragility of others' stories, those who disregard or demean the little ones of the earth, those who sacrifice and silence others. Against the odds, this is the story of such imaginative empathy, one that dares to seek understanding of whatever it is that leads others to participate in brutalizing systems. It is the *hopefulness* of the Child, which insists on the possibility of an answer. On its own, it cannot help but seem like a naivety; a yearning for the reconciliation of all things, a dream that all shall be well – *all* shall be well. It is the story that finds its way into every child-shaped space, making connections where connection does not seem possible, re-imagining what seems unimaginable. Beautiful hope rooted in the expansive solidarity of God.

On its own, this 'universal side' of the story leaves us with the impossibly uncomfortable predicament that enemies are invited to coexist in the same space, at the same table, as though the pain, anguish and terror of what some have done to others can be 'resolved'. The sheer awfulness of that prospect is why there must be another side to the story, especially when the first story is promoted by those of us with relative privileges and security, effectively minimizing the awfulness. Even though this side of the story seeks out understanding of *all* the pain, its childness must also be its Blackness, recognizing that the true costs of all that has been suffered have been borne unequally. In fact, as in O'Donnell's discussion of the toxicity of hope (in Chapter 2 above), the whole story cannot be solely characterized by hope, but must reckon with the depths of hopelessness: such as Black nihilism,[29] the rejection of any easy hope, any trite promise of resolution, any White-shaped hazy dream of peace.

On the other hand, there is the particular story – rooted in the Blackness of God's hand. It is the story of God's commitment to justice, God's love for justice, which confronts the asymmetries of the world, its imbalances, injustices, exclusions, distortions and horror. Such things are confronted in solidarity with those who bear the weight of the suffering; those who are neglected, demeaned or brutalized – all things that are easy for a person of privilege to say, with little cost to me, because they are distant from me, but which mean all too much, and resonate all too much, to many others. This second side of the story, therefore, is about identifying God's Blackness, God's Disability, God's Queerness and indeed God's Childness, not as idealized pictures, easy-to-say reversals that offer mere food for thought, or as a way of magically 'fixing' the weight of history. Rather, it is about exposing realities: the ease with which some offer their ideas without being connected to the implications or costs; the apparent straightforwardness of offering God-models without appreciating how they can be heard or felt or borne by different constituencies; the need for radical reversals if ever the different future is to take root, while recognizing that such reversals don't just happen – they involve long journeys of self-reflection, communal reflection, re-imagining, turning-around, reparation, and new commitments, by way of critical friends offering support and accountability to one another. Becoming Black. Becoming Child. Unbecoming.

But the two sides of this story cannot be held together unless the hard work of revisiting the nature of God is undertaken, which involves making those choices in how God is viewed. Of course, those of us who feel more like insiders, whether we like it or not, tend to see God-models in relatively neutral terms; they are metaphors we can fairly easily take for granted, which supposedly speak universally into all situations. But no, once we see that God-models are deeply connected with issues of power, participation and promise of different futures, we must ask ourselves: What metaphors will we choose? Prevailing metaphors, whether we see it or not, have relied on the assumptions of the giants: that Whiteness and Adultness are the norms for human life, so the norms for divine life too. Instead, it is the choice of Childness and Blackness. This commitment, seeing that even the open hand of God has a critical edge – a raging edge – especially in the face of injustice, is the means by which true, deep solidarity can come about. That is to say, *because* we choose solidarity with those with fewer privileges, against the grain of prevailing norms, the universality of the story becomes possible again, rather than a White dream.

One question that must be confronted, in the light of this disruptive metaphor of God as Child and Black, is the image of God as king. On the one hand, the kingdom of the child can take on a new way of being, as per the sermon of George MacDonald in 1867:

It is like king like subject in the kingdom of heaven ... It is the rule of kind, of nature, of deepest nature – of God. If, then, to enter into this kingdom, we must become children, the spirit of children must be its pervading spirit throughout, from lowly subject to lowliest king.[30]

Robyn Wrigley-Carr sees that, for MacDonald, this notion of childlikeness lies at the centre of the kingdom of God and of the divine nature, and therefore is fundamental to our being, as people made in God's image, citing further signs of it:[31] 'God is child-like'; Jesus 'was, is and ever shall be divinely childlike ... Childhood belongs to the divine nature'; 'it is his childlikeness that makes him our God and Father'.[32] For MacDonald, kingdom and kingship are reconfigured by the child: from top to bottom, there is a reordering. It is not quite clear, however, whether this fully reflects the subversiveness of the Blackness/Childness of God – which is more specifically in solidarity with those who are belittled by the system. After all, as we shall discuss further in Chapter 9, the 'queerness' of Christ being a king *at his birth* and *at his death*, the only times the Gospels affirm his kingship, is even more thoroughly disruptive: for this is not a king on a throne, but is an (anti-)king in the smallness of a manger and marginalized and brutalized on a cross.

This Black Child, this disruptive model for the divine life, cannot be king, except as an anti-king, because the point of God's grace and justice is that they expose us to the distorted realities within which we live, and they make possible an alternative world, where life flourishes because systems of domination are dismantled. Kingship has no part in this. The risks of aligning God with kingship are too great: when God and human authority-figures are aligned, human authority-figures become akin to God.[33] I make the same argument with regard to 'the kingdom of God'; it is why I argue that 'Holy Anarchy' is a preferable alternative: for if it is truly a 'kingdom like no other', a realm without rule-over, without domination, without models of control, then it is an anti-kingdom. It is an-archy, where the rules are changing.

I do indeed believe that this rejection of kingship ought to apply not only to God, but also to human systems of government. Even if the monarch's 'reign' is reinterpreted as 'service', or is placed in a context of institutional restraint, there remain serious problems – and arguably the model of God as Child speaks to them. Of course, there are the familiar critiques, with which I agree, about the democratic deficiencies of an unelected

Head of State, the connections with colonialism, class privilege, social elitism, deference and inherited wealth; there are also concerns for the well-being of the specific individual and the family, expected to embody an office they did not ask for, regardless of capabilities or sensibilities, and the dehumanizing role of being a media construct in a supposedly glamorous soap opera. But what of God the Black Child?

This part of the book is actually concerned with God's small-ness: wherever God is, God is small. This is a majesty not of scale and grandeur but of fragility and empathy; an open-handed God, not storing up wealth but able to receive and be affected by the wealth of others' experience, pain, joy, potential; God is in solidarity with trauma and injustice, not insulated from it; God is Child and God is Black, not the parental figure of a nation, not the supposedly neutral or 'apolitical' myth of mon-archy, but committed in attentiveness to the little ones, those belittled, those sacrificed.

I was struck, though, that the coronation of Charles III in May 2023 began with the voice of a child welcoming the king to a different kingdom – the one of God. While surrounded by much that defied this initial intent, it was a beginning with a potential for subversiveness. So too the Gospel reading, from Luke 4: 'The Spirit of the Lord is upon me, to proclaim good news to the poor.' Were these signs of God the Black Child at work? They may have been, but arguably they were co-opted by the colonial matrix of state theology in which God's king-ship and the nation's monarchy became re-entangled, and good news for the poor was clothed in quite different messaging. In fact, the predominant messaging was of a Christianity infused with monarchical ideology, where the human king was suppos-edly relativized by the divine King, one who admittedly calls for service – but it was never going to be a Christianity infused with the Magnificat, in which those on their thrones are brought down and the hungry are fed. It is interesting, after all, that the Gospels offer us other images for God but they rarely feature in our liturgies, let alone a coronation: what of the thief (1 Thes-salonians 5.2), or the burglar (Mark 3.27), or the glutton and drunkard (Matthew 11.19)? According to those, surely God the Child is disruptive of social order and bears the cost of it. According to those, God the Child is more like an anarchist, trailblazer of Holy Anarchy, than a king, protector of the status quo.

However, one critique of monarchy may be a problem for my argument: it is the suggestion that monarchy 'infantilizes' a democratic people. Here we see how a childlike image, of the infant, is deployed pejoratively; it supposes that we ought to 'grow up' and monarchy prevents us from doing so. But what, instead, if monarchy prevents us from 'growing down', because it diverts our gaze upwards, to a delusion of imperial stature, allowing monarchical subjects to presume to be above republics? True infancy, by contrast, perhaps even 'disruptive' infancy, beckons us to greater interdependence as democratic citizens, bound to one another – and this in itself can be theologically underpinned, as a republic or commonwealth of God's children, equals in freedom and accountability. It is disruptive, though, because it calls into question the delusions of imperial majesty that are wrapped up with monarchy.

Of course, any society must work at its system of government, and keep working at it, in recognition that habits and institutions are inclined to ossify; so democracy demands attentiveness, reinvigoration, renewal – and seeing ourselves as God's children, or 'children' of (or with) God the Child, keeps alive this call for dynamic revival whenever our structures become complacent, elitist or divorced from the struggles of everyday life. The Child sparks us to wonder anew: Who are we called to be? Can we be better than this? What kind of a world do we dream of? Such pursuit of alternative horizons will be explored further in Part 3.

The Black open-handedness of the Divine Child helps to keep us alert to social renewal, as well as theological renewal, because if ever people are marginalized, or expected to fit within certain norms defined by vested interests, the body politic cannot thrive. Individuals from minoritized backgrounds reaching the heights of political power are not proof that all is well; rather, they are more like the exception than the rule, often buoyed by the intersecting dynamics of class and wealth – so attentiveness to racial politics, class politics and gender politics are all necessary dimensions of a renewed public life. And each can be underpinned by the solidarity-building presence of God the Child, who holds together the universal vision of a reconciled world with the particular longing-for-justice in solidarity with those wounded by the status quo; a Child both hopeful and attuned to hopelessness; a Child both disruptive and conscious of the costs of disruption; a Child both rainbow-coloured, at one with the complexities and flows of diversity, and Black, calling out the colonized visions of childness, God, religion and society; a Child both loving the enemies of this vision and anti-monarchic, inspiring alternative visions to emerge.

Back to the adder's den

It is interesting how children can dare to do dangerous things. Of course, this is often underpinned by an ignorance of the consequences; being told that something is dangerous does not really register until the danger comes to pass. But there is also a trust there. A willingness to believe that all will be well, even when doing something that adults have become too cautious to do. An inquisitiveness: 'I wonder what will happen, if anything …' A boldness: 'I will be just fine!' A determination: 'I accept the risk!' This is quite different from models of trust that adults encourage: when they ask a child to trust them, they want them to be obedient, to fall in line and not to question.

God the Child, bearing the Blackness of the hand, disrupts adult norms; it is a choice we make to express solidarity with those who, in effect, live in danger – and Jesus' commitment to such solidarity essentially testifies to such as God the Child. The daring child. The disruptive child. Bearing the cost.

This is not to idealize such risk or danger, but rather it is to reckon with it, as honestly as possible. Snakes bite. Dangers come to pass. Systems strike back. They do not like dissent or disruption. But if we long for that world where the universal story comes to pass, where love for enemies is enacted, in religion and in society, then there must be disruption – and we turn to this more directly in Part 2.

A Pentecost hymn: Language of the stranger

'The whirlwinds of revolt will continue to shake the founda-
tions of our nation until the bright days of justice emerge.'
(Martin Luther King Jr, 'I Have a Dream' speech, 1963)

God, pouring out your spirit on your daughters
and on your sons, on all flesh young and old,
you spark in us the dream to keep on dreaming;
help us desire a future yet more bold:

Where even now black people must seek justice
while white men scorn the cries of 'I can't breathe',
when, faced with systems, men and women protest,
teach us to dream: let everyone be free!

God, breezing through the gaps in our security,
shaking foundations keeping us apart,
you spark in us a whirlwind of awareness;
help us pursue the future that you start:

Where people suffer prejudice and hatred
and old suspicions damage our goodwill,
where others' needs are minimized or twisted,
teach us to dream that life shall be fulfilled!

God, burning bright in faith that calls us outwards
led by your spirit's empathetic ways,
help us to hear, in language of the stranger,
dreams that combine to shape the coming days.

(Graham Adams, 2020)
Suggested tune: *Lord for the years*

Questions

1 To say 'God is Child' is not simply to think a bit differently about God. It is to make an argument for liberation, just as 'God is Black' is a challenge to the norms and structures that go hand in hand with prevailing Whiteness. What do you think about this?

2 How does the Blackness of God the Child expose and confront systems that defend vested interests?

3 How does the Blackness of God the Child speak to alternative visions, not only in theology, but in politics? How could it encourage deeper mutuality between us as equal children of God?

Notes

1 Walter Mignolo speaks of the 'colonial matrix of power' in Walter Mignolo, 2012, 'Decolonizing Western Epistemologies/Building Decolonial Epistemologies', in Ada María Isasi-Díaz and Eduardo Mendieta (eds), *Decolonizing Epistemologies: Latina/o Theology and Philosophy*, New York: Fordham Press, pp. 27–8. I make it more explicitly about 'adult power'. See also p. 101.

2 However, as Anthony Reddie acknowledges, the great challenge for Black theology is the sheer persistence of Black oppression, raising questions about the efficacy of God's liberating power: Anthony G. Reddie, 2008, 'What Is the Point of This? A Practical Black Theology Exploration of Suffering and Theodicy', in Anthony G. Reddie, *Working Against the Grain: Reimagining Black Theology in the 21st Century*, London: Equinox, pp. 172–87. Ultimately, for James Cone, it comes down to faith, as James A. Calloway identified, in 2020, in '"To Struggle Up a Never-Ending Stair": Theodicy and the Failure it Gifts to Black Theology', *Black Theology: An International Journal*, 18(3), pp. 223–45, specifically pp. 239–40.

3 Nancy Eiesland, 1994, *The Disabled God: Toward a Liberatory Theology of Disability*, Nashville, TN: Abingdon.

4 Marcella Althaus-Reid, 2003, *The Queer God (God the Homosexual)*, London: Routledge.

5 James H. Cone, 1997, *God of the Oppressed*, rev. edn, Maryknoll,

NY: Orbis, p. 136, identifying those who universalize their experience, on the basis of particular interests.

6 Cone, *God of the Oppressed*, p. 63: 'There is no place in black theology for a colorless God in a society where human beings suffer precisely because of their color.' Anthony Reddie also affirms that others had made the assertion of God's Blackness previously: Henry McNeal Turner, who said 'God is a Negro' (1898), and Marcus Garvey (1924); Anthony G. Reddie, 2022, *Introducing James H. Cone: A Personal Exploration*, London: SCM Press, pp. 48–9.

7 James Cone, 2010, *A Black Theology of Liberation*, Maryknoll, NY: Orbis, p. 63.

8 Reddie, *Introducing Cone*, p. 47.

9 See R. L. Stollar, 2016, 'Using vs Liberating Children: How Child Theology Differs from Child Liberation Theology', 26 April, https://rlstollar.com/2016/04/26/using-vs-liberating-children-how-child-theology-differs-from-child-liberation-theology/?amp=1 (accessed 13.9.23). See also R. L. Stollar, 2023, *The Kingdom of Children: A Liberation Theology*, Grand Rapids, MI: Eerdmans.

10 Rohan P. Gideon, 2021, 'Soteriology and Children's Vulnerabilities and Agency', in Marcia J. Bunge (ed.), *Child Theology: Diverse Methods and Global Perspectives*, Maryknoll, NY: Orbis, pp. 90, 104–6.

11 Anne Richards, 2013, *Children in the Bible: A Fresh Approach*, London: SPCK, 2013, p. 103.

12 John Baxter-Brown, 2014, 'Identities: Theology, Mission and Child in the Upside-Down Kingdom', in Bill Prevette et al. (eds), *Theology, Mission and Child: Global Perspectives*, Oxford: Regnum, 2014, p. 161.

13 Baxter-Brown, 'Identities', pp. 153–4.

14 Aamna Mohdin, 2022, '"They saw me as calculating, not a child": how adultification leads to black children being treated as criminals', *The Guardian*, 5 July, https://www.theguardian.com/society/2022/jul/05/they-saw-me-as-calculating-not-a-child-how-adultification-leads-to-black-children-being-treated-as-criminals (accessed 1.8.23).

15 Reddie, *Introducing Cone*, p. 46.

16 Reddie, *Introducing Cone*, p. 46.

17 Reddie is explicit, for instance, that White Christianity 'is not a benign phenomenon … [but] a violent religion', p. 45; also, Anthony G. Reddie, 2020, 'Reassessing the Inculcation of an Anti-Racist Ethic for Christian Ministry: From Racism Awareness to Deconstructing Whiteness', *Religions*, 11(10), p. 497.

18 Reddie, *Introducing Cone*, p. 51.

19 Reddie, *Introducing Cone*, p. 52.

20 Cited in Klippies Kritzinger, 1988, 'Black Theology – Challenge to Mission', doctoral thesis, Pretoria: University of South Africa, p. 201.

21 Rachel Starr, 2023, 'Unbecoming: Reflections on the Work of a White Theologian', in Anthony G. Reddie and Carol Troupe (eds), *Deconstructing Whiteness, Empire and Mission*, London: SCM Press, p. 239.

22 Lisa Isherwood, 1999, *Liberating Christ: Exploring the Christologies of Contemporary Liberation Movements*, Cleveland, OH: Pilgrim Press, p. 35.

23 Selina Stone and Fr Simon Cuff, 2022, 'Race, Inclusion and Social Justice in the British Church: A Review', *Studies in Christian Ethics*, 35(3), pp. 622–32.

24 Graham Adams, 2022, *Holy Anarchy: Dismantling Domination, Embodying Community, Loving Strangeness*, London: SCM Press, p. 26.

25 Cone, *God of the Oppressed*, p. 136.

26 We return to this in Chapter 8, in the context of theological education.

27 Al Barrett and Ruth Harley, 2023, '"Holding the Space": Troubling "the Facilitating Obsession of Whiteness"', in Reddie and Troupe (eds), *Deconstructing Whiteness, Empire and Mission*, pp. 281–2: 'facilitating obsession of whiteness' as named by Willie James Jennings.

28 See Néstor Míguez, Joerg Rieger and Jung Mo Sung, 2009, *Beyond the Spirit of Empire*, London: SCM Press, p. 133. See also Jung Mo Sung, 2007, *Desire, Market and Religion*, London: SCM Press, pp. 49–50, 91, 95–6, 98 ('sacrificialism').

29 Calvin L. Warren, 2015, 'Black Nihilism and the Politics of Hope', first appeared in *The New Centennial Review*, 15(1), Spring, http://docplayer.net/48679084-Black-nihilism-and-the-politics-of-hope-calvin-warren.html#show_full_text (accessed 13.9.23).

30 George MacDonald, 2007, 'The Child in the Midst', in George MacDonald, *Unspoken Sermons*, New York: Cosimo Classics (originally published 1867), pp. 14, 15.

31 Robyn Wrigley-Carr, 2018, 'Proclaiming and Cultivating 'Childlikeness': A Subversive Thread in Christian Anthropology', *International Journal of Children's Spirituality*, 23(1), pp. 45–52.

32 MacDonald, *Unspoken Sermons*, pp. 18, 19, 24.

33 See, for example, Mary Daly, 1992, *Beyond God the Father: Toward a Philosophy of Women's Liberation*, Boston, MA: Beacon Press.

PART 2

However God Acts, God is Weak

How powerful is God? Prevailing models of God certainly tend to affirm that God is 'almighty', able to do anything. It seems to be important, because it explains the scale and wonder of the universe, created by an agency with such power; but it is also because we want to know that any other kinds of power in the world are relative in comparison with God: they may seem to hold sway for now, but they are temporary or can be put in their place. After all, God's power is needed for God to do justice, and the doing of justice is a demonstration of God's love for all. That is to say, because God is perfect love, God's justice will follow, exercised through good power, well used. So God's power matters – for creation and for salvation/liberation – because without God's power the forces of domination, cruelty, injustice, disease and indifference will prevail.

There are, of course, theologies that question this, not least in the light of the suffering in the world.[1] If God is so powerful, why wait to act, or why act so inconsistently? Why not act now, in the face of so many instances of overwhelming brutality – and wherever an individual suffers so horribly? The usual answer is freedom: creation needs its freedom. We are free to choose right and to choose wrong. Sin, after all, is a clear and present reality, and its presence gives us choices. But this argument can be confusing for at least two reasons: first, many people's freedom is limited, precisely because of the structures of sin, which have asymmetrical impacts. Many people's choices are hugely inhibited due to the inequities in the world, where those with many more privileges have more freedom, more choice, but rarely exercise it to tip the balance towards a more just world of greater freedom for all. So even if our freedom is meant to be the explanation for how we respond to the inequitable distribution of suffering, it is a poor explanation. Those who suffer most have limited freedom to overcome it, in which case why would God not help those who suffer in such unfreedom? Why would God not help those who suffer through no fault of their own? The answer, we are told, is that God 'is' helping them, slowly, through the outworkings of salvation and the call for others to participate with God in securing freedom for all. But this is certainly a slow process, and sometimes it goes backwards. Is it a good argument? What use is it, to someone suffering in catastrophic climate disasters, or in domestic violence or war, that the outworkings of salvation are in process – if God *could* do more but chooses not to?

Second, the Christian tradition itself teaches that our capacity to choose the good is impeded by sin; in other words, we are fighting an uphill struggle, in terms of our freedom to choose well, because we do not even know what we are doing – our 'will' is infected, so what exactly is the nature of our freedom? Surely God should intervene with God's power more frequently to aid us? The answer, again we are told, is that we can trust in the mystery of God's justice, which has defeated the power of sin, cosmically, even if the effects of this are not yet fully realized; and God also forgives us for being overcome by sin, because God graciously understands our weakness and loves us. But again: is this a good argument? If our choice matters, why is it so impeded? Why is our capacity to use our freedom well so distorted? We are told that God restrains God's actions out of due regard for our freedom, and yet our freedom is itself corrupted, so God ought to act.

There are obviously many books written on these issues and conundrums, but what happens if we bring God the Child to bear on them? How does God's power look different? How does this change the focus, the assumptions and the effects? This part of the book explores these questions.

In Chapter 4, I use the image of the chaos-event to revisit the nature of God's power as childlike; its smallness and weakness imply a different model that is nevertheless capable of, or at least makes possible, considerable disruptions and transformations, like a child's chaotic and subversive power.[2] Chapter 5 then considers what this means for divine justice, suggesting that the image of playfulness may be helpful here, because of its disruption of the status quo. I explore this in particular in terms of 'degrowth', an economic and ecological proposal for downsizing imperial hubris and healing the Earth. In Chapter 6, much as I brought Blackness to bear on the image of the open palm in Chapter 3, I ask how Disability theologies may help us to understand divine agency in contexts of injustice: how power is exercised but also limited. As in Part 1, the focus overall is to see what emerges when Adult theology is subverted, here specifically by the 'weakness' of childlike power.

Notes

1 See, for example, Thomas Jay Oord, 2023, *The Death of Omnipotence and Birth of Amipotence*, Grasmere, ID: SacraSage Press.

2 After all, as R. L. Stollar argues, in disagreement with Janet Pais, children are not powerless – and to believe they are is 'adultist'. He notes that Pais believes it is for adults to fight for children's rights on their behalf, due to their powerlessness. See R. L. Stollar, 1991, *Suffer the Children: A Theology of Liberation by a Victim of Child Abuse*, Mahwah, NJ: Paulist Press, pp. 16–17. Stollar argues instead that children are only powerless *relative to adults*, that they are indeed disempowered by adults, but that they also have, or certainly *can* have, all kinds of power – they can educate themselves, advocate, protest, organize, use social media, share stories, raise money, report abuse, engage in community service, run for school office. 'In short, children can be advocates, revolutionaries, and world-changers just as much as adults!' Thus, children, and indeed God the Child, are not powerless but subversively powerful. See R. L. Stollar, 2022, 'Children are not Powerless: A Disagreement with Janet Pais', 9 October, https://rlstollar.com/2022/10/09/children-are-not-powerless-a-disagreement-with-janet-pais/?amp=1 (accessed 13.09.23).

4

God the Chaos-event

'Truly I tell you, if you have faith the size of a mustard seed,
you will say to this mountain, "Move from here to there",
and it will move; and nothing will be impossible for you.'
(Matthew 17.20–21)

God the Child, mover of mountains

The Bullies say I'm nothing. They say I'm good for nothing.
They say I'm weak and feeble.

Maybe they're right, maybe I've come to believe them,
maybe I'm not strong enough for anything.

But deep down, I know they're wrong. They don't see it.
They can't see it. They don't want to.

I've got a kind of power they may never accept or understand.

It's not the kind of power to put other people's heads
against a wall or to knock air out of them.

Well, maybe it could knock the air out of them, but not
through force.

Instead, it's the kind of power that stops people in their
tracks, takes their breath away, almost because it doesn't seem
possible: like the flutter of a fragile wing, like the whisper of
the wind in the trees, like a flash in the corner of your eye, it's
a power that distracts from the routines and inertia of normal
life – the smallest of sparks, capable of igniting the greatest of
fires – not making it happen, but making it possible.

This is my power: teasing a hand or a heart open, gracing
a cheek with a tear of solidarity, stirring the senses to alert-

ness; even where stronger powers would close it down, still it erupts in the cracks.

Like a teaspoon of yeast.

Like a tiny seed.

An infant's tantrum, bringer of chaos.

Raw and wild.

Or the gentlest catching of eye-contact

And a smile.

And those who stamp their authority find themselves stamping on a Lego brick.

Those who command or demand respect find themselves surrounded by disarming laughter.

Those who come at me with fists, swords, empires – they see I've written on their wall.

And mountains move.

Un-misunderstanding children

It may seem a ridiculous word: un-misunderstanding. But I'm reminded that children make up words, and my students will have noticed that I do too. It's a part of grasping after the truth that won't be grasped. After all, merely saying 'understanding children' wouldn't capture what's involved. There is a deep-rooted misunderstanding of children, shaped on the one hand by Victorian mindsets and behaviour, that needs to be *un*done, *un*learned, but also by the context of global capitalism and a culture of consumption. While these issues are increasingly identified and being dismantled, we need to be as explicit about these things as possible, even in ways that may be new.

I discussed this elsewhere, where I began to wonder what it might mean to conceive of Jesus as 'God the Child', the first-born of God's new creation. (That is, before I could see that God's childness is bigger than Jesus.) There, I also suggested we could think of other characters, like Thomas, as children, and how stories can take on a different life when seen through the experience of childhood. To set the scene, though, I identified this pincer-attack on current notions of childness (at least in the West, and possibly more widely as a result of globalizing forces) – on the one hand, the idealization or romanticization of childhood, a period of life to be kept as innocent as possible, uncorrupted, trusting, simple; and on the other, the commodification of childhood, its identifying by the global market as a target for advertising, the early stages of conditioning people as economic agents. This 'ambivalence', between the celebrated innocence of children and their role as consumers, is also named and examined by Joyce Ann Mercer, for example, who examines the relationship between what she calls 'clean children' and 'dirty money'.[1] In those two dimensions, we see the conflicts to which children are subjected – to be as un-adult-like as possible, clean and supposedly unconditioned, yet on the other hand to begin to play their part in the economy of consumption, growing quickly into the adults they must be. Educational environments witness to this conflict within adult expectations – first, accused of defying children's innocence by helping them to learn things that adults may not be ready for them to learn – for example, matters such as sex and sexuality – while second, being under pressure to make children as 'useful' for the economy as possible.

But it is, of course, the role of religion that concerns me here: our dominant interpretations of child-centred texts tend to justify and fuel these conflicts. Key texts are Mark 10.15 – 'receive the kingdom of God as a little child' – and Matthew 18.3 – 'change and become like children'. Under the influence of Victorian ideals, we assume that receiving like a child or becoming like a child must entail being as innocent and trusting as possible. It is a compliant child, a well-behaved child; the child in the Christmas carol, 'mild, obedient, good as he'; the child who shows what it means to bear the *adult's* longing for innocence, unaffected by the corruption and complexity of the wider world. At the same time, this quiet compliance encourages the child to be schooled into an adult world: learn the ropes, play your part, grow into the understanding that adults have. After all, Paul implies that we too should leave 'childish ways' behind (1 Corinthians 13.11); so we know and appreciate that the time comes when all that we have learned as children will be put into practice as mature adults. This is why we tend to teach them 'our' way of understanding the faith, morality, as well as communion; so that their early innocence blossoms into an unquestioning acceptance of what adults deem to be true. It is a dangerous exploitation of innocence.[2]

There is this perfect tension: we expect children to be children as long as possible, but of a certain sort – trusting, naïve, simple-minded – while also schooling them into becoming adults who give up childish ways and take their place in the grand story, whether it is the religious tradition or indeed the economy.

Both parts of this pincer-attack on the truthfulness of child-likeness are challenged by the demands of God the Child, an alternative model of power – in fact, the firstborn of a subversive vision, which turns both religion and economics upside-down.[3] First, the innocence of childlikeness is called into question: both because reality itself tells us that children know far more about the world than we care to admit, whether because they sit on the stairs and listen, or suffer its brutalities, or they simply notice, and because Jesus himself was not exhorting innocence but alertness to receive God's new realm *as a little one at the bottom of the pile*. That is, children in his day were among 'the least', so for adults to receive this new world as children is to rediscover what it means to be in solidarity with all who are belittled, which cannot involve innocence but, instead, stark alertness to the ways of the world.

Were children only trusting, they might never ask questions, push the boundaries or disobey, but they are excellent interrogators, seeing through flimsy adult attempts to close down an awkward conversation; they see unfairness; they see connections between humans and nature; they see wonder and harm; they imagine alternatives. On the one hand, the idealization of childhood has a ring of truth, because it allows children to be unconditioned by the world views of adults, to dream dreams but, on the other, it expects those dreams to stay in their childish place. By contrast, God the Child calls them forth, encourages them, spurs them on.

Second, then, the expectation that children will come to play their part as adults in the prevailing order, whether religious or economic, is also profoundly challenged by God the Child. For this divine agency is disruptive, question-pursuing, adventurously rebellious – in the face of the suffering we acknowledged above in the introduction to Part 2. It is not about being held in our place, but is in fact a rising up against prevailing norms and expectations. Wanda Deifelt speaks of the child as 'knowing'; one who 'confronts adults' and does so with their 'immense power'.[4]

So the work continues – to un-misunderstand children; not to see them as current or future defenders of an existing empire, but to doubt it, to question it, to re-imagine the world, to colour outside of the lines that have been given us by expectant adults, to ask 'Why? Why? Why?' in the face of supposed inevitabilities and also 'Why not?' when confronted with all the difficulties involved in transformation.

But the question remains: what is the nature of this power, this disruptive agency, in the face of such systems and expectations? How, exactly, does God the Child subvert, and encourage further subversions of, the status quo?

The colonial matrix of adult power

The first thing that this power consists of is its revelation of reality: it helps us to see the system more fully. In the terms of Part 1, the 'open hand' of God the Child is capable of revealing what we do not want to see; like an open hand as space in which things come to light, and redirecting our gaze towards the dynamics that prevail, the suffering obscured in small spaces, the yearning for deeper solidarity. It is an open hand and a Black hand, illuminating the asymmetric structures – systems of racism, sexism, classism, ableism, homophobia, transphobia, the exploitation of the Earth, adultism and more. It is a hand that, in its smallness, its fragility, its presence in and among the belittled, dares to show us reality and inspires us to glimpse and pursue its transformation.

Walter Mignolo speaks of the 'colonial matrix of power':[5] a set of forces that hold the world a certain way. All sorts of voices offer slightly different versions of this analysis, many of which I affirmed in *Holy Anarchy* but, as elsewhere, I also add to Mignolo's phrase by suggesting it is primarily a 'colonial matrix of *adult* power':[6] a colonial matrix designed by adults, serving the interests of adults. Of course, not all adults are equally responsible; certainly not all adults in equal measure, because the colonial matrix is profoundly asymmetric, or skewed towards the securities of some at the expense of the many; but the point remains that children are not involved in developing or affecting this matrix of power. They are, instead, subjected to it – not least its expectations of their innocence and of their growth into maturing economic agents.

The first art and task of this disruptive power – that of God the Child – is to draw this colonial matrix to our attention. We live in a world of stark inequalities and inequities, no matter how often we are told that its prevailing norms and forms are inevitable, natural or just.

Walter Brueggemann writes how God, through scripture, exposes the frameworks of the world and offers an alternative frame of reference[7] – but what if this 'alternative' is particularly understood in terms of the contrast between adult ways and child ways? Again, this is not to idealize childhood, as though 'adult' is always wrong or bad and 'child' is always right or good; rather, it is – as I said previously – to affirm particular possibilities that arise when the nature of God and God's power and agency are seen in childlike terms.

Where the system is one of empire, of overbearing structures and patterns, powers of domination and control, and where God is seen in similar terms, even if only implicitly, as the One 'in charge' – whose plan is being slowly but somehow system-atically put into force – by contrast 'God the Child' shows us a different way. Where the system is a mountain, representing the Temple Mount, the seat of religious and political authority and power in Jesus' day, the Temple-State behind which even the Roman empire could operate, by contrast God the Child is like a mustard seed. Al Barrett and Ruth Harley powerfully elaborate the deviance of this image;[8] not clean and tidy, but like an infestation (as Andrew Shanks also notes[9]), a weed that cannot be easily removed, a persistent, defiant plant that grows and becomes a sanctuary for wild birds, those who might otherwise have no space for refuge. This small seed becomes the very means by which the foundations of the colonial matrix of adult power are destabilized. It is, once again, an excellent illustration of the theological significance of chaos theory.

Chaos

I have referred to chaos theory elsewhere.[10] I readily acknowledge that my engagement with the theory is not as thorough as it might be; rather, I take a key feature of the mathematical theory and run with it, seeing its connections with the disruptive but 'weak' nature of divine agency. Essentially, it is about the unpredictable but logical consequences of some small events, notably in terms of their capacity to lead to much larger and widespread effects. Basically, my argument is that God's power is not 'strong' as we would understand the word 'strong'; it is not the kind of capacity that can impose its will on the atoms, molecules, organisms and individual wills of the creaturely universe. Rather, it is more like a butterfly fluttering its wings; a fragile wisp of an event, which nevertheless can have far-reaching impact, as one thing leads to another, and a wave of responses ensues from the gentlest of beginnings.

This is how the revelatory power of the open hand operates. It stirs us. It draws our attention to reality. It elicits an awakening in us. It invites us to notice, to care, to respond. It does not 'make' it happen, but flutters past us, distracting us from the norms and routines that otherwise occupy us, and goes on its way, like a wind blowing where it will, but no gale-force wind; rather, it is a breeze, nonetheless capable of initiating unpredictable effects – in us, in communities, in people unlike us but who are also stirred.

It is chaos-power. God as chaos-event. God the Child evoking a response with consequences it does not know – though we come to the question of knowledge in Part 3. Here, the issue is that God cannot determine the consequences, even if God may well desire them. It is divine desire calling out to creaturely desire, trusting that there may be an echo of it in our own fragile agency. We find ourselves committing to do something that reflects the will of the one who stirs us to life and action, but God did not control us into doing it. This is why so often we do not do the thing, or creaturely desires are not redirected towards the cause in question: God is not the sort of agency with the kind of power necessary to guarantee the proper response, so seeks out ever-new ways to inspire and nudge and invite, while remaining butterfly-like.

Or, indeed, childlike.

After all, the point I am seeking to make here is that this chaos-power is especially pertinent to the project of God the Child. It does not take much to see the truth of the Child as bringer of chaos: the seemingly 'small event' that prompts, or stirs, or calls forth, such wide-ranging and logical though unpredictable consequences. The connection between chaos theory and complexity theory helps to elaborate the point, because not only does the presence of the child evoke far larger repercussions, like a butterfly leading to a hurricane but, as in complexity theory, the pre-existing system and its equilibrium (in whatever sense there may be an equilibrium) is destabilized and there is no possibility of returning to how things were. This is true not only of a child, but of God the Child.

The advent of God the Child, their coming into any situation or network, whether in history or here and now, is always a disruption, no matter how small and seemingly unnoticed the event may be. Both as open hand and chaos-event, God the Child breathes into the smallest of cracks in our world, illuminating what is there, including the substructures of the colonial matrix of power, and somehow nothing can be the same again. Like yeast; like a mustard seed; like buried treasure, God the Child may be 'only' a chaos-event, weak in contrast to brute force, but their repercussions are potentially uncontainable. They are also interdependent repercussions; that is, as Deifelt puts it: 'Recognizing our own vulnerability and weakness allows us to come to terms with and accept the weakness of others'[11] – and there is power in this; the power of empathy, deepened through the attentiveness of the open hand, enabling solidarities to grow.

Though my previous efforts to explain God the Child have focused on Jesus as its embodiment, my argument in this book is broader than that: I am proposing that there are interesting, creative and disruptive possibilities that flow from thoroughly re-focusing on *God as Child* – and here, it is the reappraisal of divine power that follows from that, and divine power in its relation with others. But it is worth noting what this might mean particularly for how we view Jesus of Nazareth. First, I reiterate the model of embodiment: Jesus embodies God the Child, by showing us – in fact, *living* for us – what the childness or childlikeness of God means. It is bold and adventurous, to which I return in Part 3, but Part 1 was about the solidarity of the child, in the places of smallness, in the midst of the cries, and here in Part 2 it is about the disruptiveness of the child. Surely we can see Jesus as disruptive; his embodying of God the Child demonstrates for us how divine agency, as chaos-event, calls the status quo into question. It causes us to notice what we might otherwise not notice; to care; to respond. It helps us to recognize the colonial matrix of (adult) power, which impinges on and harms the dignity of so many – and it disrupts these very structures.

But second, it may be helpful to think of Jesus not only as embodying God the Child, but as their friend. For Jesus does not do it all. He does not exhaust the extent of God the Child. In fact, in John's Gospel he tells us that we will do greater works than him (John 14.12) – because his desire, his spirit, his vision is to remain the best of friends with God the Child, no matter who enacts the Child's desires. It is a loyalty that will not be broken; a loyalty that affirms and celebrates our own agency, our own contributions to the further embodying and befriending of God the Child. In Jesus we see the best friend of God the Child, since he looks beyond his own embodiment of it, and delights, like Divine Wisdom, in all God's creation (Proverbs 8.31) – in our potential to be chaos-events to one another, and to participate with him, our friend, and the friend of God the Child, in loving new creation into being.

God the Child, the original chaos-event, called forth its own embodiment in Jesus, without controlling it; rather, it affirmed Jesus' own response to the call. Then Jesus, through embodying it though not exhausting or containing it, reflected its chaos-power, its propensity to call forth other reflections, other chaos-events, other embodiments: so we find ourselves knit together in a mutual ecology of life, of friends, of faithful pursuers of this new reality. Like God the Child, bringer of chaos, dreamer of Holy Anarchy – the new realm where the colonial matrix of power is disrupted and transformed – Jesus too desires and inspires such 'chaos-ing'; and, through us, the reverberations continue.

But third, one more image for Jesus' relationship with God the Child: not only embodying it; not only befriending it; but Jesus as the 'kite-flyer' of God the Child, helping us to see its beauty and movement. This re-emerges implicitly in Part 3, where we discover God the Child seeking horizons out of boundless curiosity, but here, in relation to divine power, the point is that even though the affinity between God (as Child) and Jesus is distinctly integrated, there is also always space for some ambiguity in the relationship – again because of Jesus not exhausting the extent of God the Child. What Jesus also does is discern the Spirit, the breath, the wind, as small and gentle as it may be or as fierce and formidable as it becomes through the reverberations of deeper 'chaos-ing'; Jesus waits like a kite-flyer, patiently praying for the moments when he will be caught up in its play, but also praying to be free from it and its demands because of the cost. As God the Child stirs life and possibility, calling forth and evoking even breath itself, the wind of hope and healing, this flow of fresh air, must then be made visible, its movement becoming evident when the kite of our desires, attitudes and actions reflects it.

The advantage of this image is that the power is subtle: you cannot force a kite to fly; it is the wind that takes it, but we must partner with it. We cannot fully embody this childlike wind, this energy, this movement, but we can to some extent learn to desire what it desires. We can be its friend, as Jesus was/is the best friend for ever of God the Child, the chaos-event of all chaos-events, stirring, eliciting, inviting, moving ... but this same disruptive energy, breezing through cracks and nudging prison doors open, is also like the wind that must be made visible by our imperfect but gloriously receptive kite-flying, rising and falling on the currents of chaos.

Growing downwards

Dear God,
What does this mean for us?
You are bread and baker, you are lamb and shepherd,
But you are also child and midwife,
Stranger and friend;
For you come to us, in ways that are both familiar and new,
Disrupting what we take for granted,
Taking root among us, like a weed that will not go away,
Making some of our safety feel oddly dangerous
While giving sanctuary to those with nowhere to place
    their head.
So come again, bring your chaos,
Up-end our securities, destabilize our foundations,
Even as a small event in an overbearing world;
Come, in your smallness, till we see more clearly the scale of
    the challenge:
The bread that is stone, the shepherds that neglect their sheep,
The children that play tunes but are ignored;
Come, bring your chaos, do your worst,
Like a wind that carries our hopelessness while nourishing
    hope,
and help us, like Jesus, to fly kites that show your currents
flowing towards a different kind of world
where those on their thrones are brought low
and the little, the least, the last, the lost are fed at your party;
so come, bring your chaos,
till we learn to grow downwards, to see the world from
    lower down
while flying these bold kites, which dip and dive,

and fall and rise;
come, bring your chaos, that we may bring our own
in pursuit of your desires
on earth as in your dreams.

Hymn: Water-people

This hymn references chaos, taking its cue from the Revd Prof
Upolu Vaai, Principal of Pacific Theological College, whose plea
for the oceans to be safeguarded includes a poignant yearning
for the 'wild, unruly chaos' of the Spirit. Reflecting on it, and
on the 'blue theology' surrounding it, I suggest our faith may
best be understood in terms of water rather than land, and yet
we are inclined to 'landed' ways of thinking and behaving, as
though our faith is more about firm foundations than the risk,
fluidity and connectivity of water. There is, in fact, something
childlike about responding to the call of water.

God of terrain and oceans
and every shade of sky,
we are such landed people:
on earth we sing and cry;
informed by what's beneath us,
our faith seeks solid ground –
not like the shape of water,
which spills and slips around.

And yet we're torn between them:
we seek security,
a world of firm foundations –
but listen to the sea:
its wild, unruly chaos*
inspires us and enthrals,
for while the land upholds us,
your living water calls.

---

* The phrase is from Upolu Vaai's prayer for the ocean: https://ptc.
ac.fj/a-call-for-the-ocean/.

In Christ, we're water-people
baptized into your grace,
which flows to reconnect us –
walls crumble without trace.
This pale blue dot** of water,
where streams of justice flow,
sees faith, like shorelines, moving
and floods of love shall grow.

(Graham Adams, 2023)
Suggested tunes: *King's Lynn, Penlan, Thornbury*

Questions

1 I argue that the system conditions us to expect children to be innocent, on the one hand, and people who are learning to be economic agents, on the other – in both cases, a denial of the wholeness of childhood. Can you see how God the Child disrupts these expectations?

2 How might God as Child expose and subvert the colonial matrix of adult power – this system that maintains the prevailing dynamics of power?

3 What do you make of the chaos-event of God the Child? Is it a helpful or difficult way of making sense of how God acts and encourages us to act?

4 What of Jesus as embodiment of God the Child, as best friend of God the Child, and as kite-flyer of God the Child? What does each image offer – to our faith and our discipleship?

** This alludes to Carl Sagan's depiction of Earth as the 'pale blue dot', as seen from *Voyager 2*, in 1990, when it was four billion miles away from us. This is, after all, the blue planet.

Notes

1 Joyce Ann Mercer, 2005, *Welcoming Children: A Practical Theology of Childhood*, St Louis, MO: Chalice Press, pp. 73–6.

2 R. L. Stollar in 2023 warns that this notion of innocence is indeed exploited and misused by adults, especially – in this context – by the Christian Right, in order to push an anti-LGBTQI+ agenda: 'How the Right Perverts and Weaponizes Child Protection', 27 June, https://rlstollar.com/2023/06/27/how-the-right-perverts-and-weaponizes-child-protection/?amp=1 (accessed 18.09.23). Elsewhere he argues that child protection is indeed for all God's children, using intersectionality to argue against those who would denigrate the needs and rights of certain groups: R. L. Stollar, 2016, 'Child Protection is for All God's Children', *Patheos*, 8 September, https://www.patheos.com/blogs/unfundamentalistparenting/2016/09/child-protection-is-for-all-gods-children/ (accessed 18.09.23).

3 See Wanda Deifelt, 2021, 'The God-Child Paradigm and Paradoxes of the Incarnation', in Marcia J. Bunge (ed.), *Child Theology: Diverse Methods and Global Perspectives*, Maryknoll, NY: Orbis, p. 76: 'The God-Child paradigm temporarily upends social structures and expectations'; and, p. 77, '[b]y becoming a child, God changed the power dynamics and suspended social hierarchies'. Here we see that, while Deifelt does indeed affirm the political significance of divine childness, its temporariness differs from my argument about the perpetual childlikeness of the divine.

4 Deifelt, 'God-Child Paradigm', p. 87.

5 Walter Mignolo, 2012, 'Decolonizing Western Epistemologies/Building Decolonial Epistemologies', in Ada María Isasi-Díaz and Eduardo Mendieta (eds), *Decolonizing Epistemologies: Latina/o Theology and Philosophy*, New York: Fordham Press, pp. 27–8.

6 See Graham Adams, 2024 (forthcoming), 'Mission in the Colonial Matrix of Adult Power: Child-centredness as Way, Truth, Life!', in Benjamin Aldous, Harvey Kwiyani, Peniel Rajkumar and Victoria Turner (eds), *'Lived' Mission in 21st Century Britain: Ecumenical and Postcolonial Perspectives*, London: SCM Press; emphasis in original.

7 Walter Brueggemann, 2009, *Redescribing Reality: What We Do When We Read the Bible*, London: SCM Press, p. 5.

8 Al Barrett and Ruth Harley, 2020, *Being Interrupted: Re-Imagining the Church's Mission from the Outside*, London: SCM Press, pp. 121–2.

9 Andrew Shanks, 2015, *Hegel Versus 'InterFaith Dialogue': A General Theory of True Xenophilia*, New York: Cambridge University Press, pp. 164–5.

10 Graham Adams, 2019, *Theology of Religions: Through the Lens of 'Truth-as-Openness'*, Leiden: Brill, p. 65; 2022, *Holy Anarchy: Dismantling Domination, Embodying Community, Loving Strangeness*, London: SCM Press, p. 109; and 2023, 'Glimpses of God's Dis/Abled Domain: Rising Up against Empire in Small Steps/Huge Leaps', in Jione Havea (ed.), *Dissensions and Tenacity: Doing Theology with Nerves*, Lanham, MD: Lexington, pp. 173–4.

11 Deifelt, 'God-Child Paradigm', p. 81.

5

Justice as Playfulness

Now the word of the LORD came to me saying,
'Before I formed you in the womb I knew you,
and before you were born I consecrated you;
I appointed you a prophet to the nations.'
Then I said, 'Ah, Lord GOD! Truly I do not know how to
speak, for I am only a boy.'
But the LORD said to me,
'Do not say, "I am only a boy";
for you shall go to all to whom I send you,
and you shall speak whatever I command you.
Do not be afraid of them,
for I am with you to deliver you,
says the LORD.'
Then the LORD put out his hand and touched my mouth;
and the LORD said to me,
'Now I have put my words in your mouth.
See, today I appoint you over nations and over kingdoms,
to pluck up and to pull down,
to destroy and to overthrow,
to build and to plant.'
(Jeremiah 1.4–10)

Only

But I'm only a child. So what can I do?
Well, you can overthrow.
You can pull up the roots.
You can destroy the structures built by the grown-ups.
You can overturn the plans that keep things the way they are.
That's what you can do.

But how can I do this? Won't they stop me?
They might.
They'll certainly try.
But you're only a child.
They won't expect it.
It's not the sort of power they anticipate.
The power of play.
It's what you bring.
It's who you are.
It unsettles them.
It disarms their insecurity.

But I'm only a child.
Exactly.
'Only.'
A Child.

Connections

The story of Jeremiah is that God begins by putting the proph-et's childness at the centre: it is in his very childness that the call to turn the world upside-down takes root. This is what we also see when Jesus put a child 'among them', at the centre (Mark 9.36). However, I have not yet outlined the different movements in theology that are concerned with the place of children. I wanted, first, to establish that my approach to God *as* Child has had its own trajectory, emerging most crucially from the challenge of empire and its colonial matrix of adult power,[1] and how God's anti-empire (anti-kingdom, or Holy Anarchy) is distinctly focused on smallness, encapsulated by the way of childlikeness. But I need to locate this more explic-itly in relation to other movements, which will help to sharpen my argument, especially in terms of its concern for justice. The insight of Ryan Stollar is critical in this regard.

Stollar notes that there are three different movements – the Theology of Childhood (TOC), the Child Theology Movement (CTM) and Child Liberation Theology (CLT).[2] In fact, TOC is a collection of approaches that focus on children in themselves, what is happening theologically within the lives, experiences and agency of children, and how better to encourage their spirituality. It is a key resource for understanding the intrinsic value of children. However, I am not directly drawing from it, as such, but at least implicitly (if inadequately) affirming some of its assumptions: that children matter as children, and if adults claim to be interested in being childlike, they should not edit or romanticize such rich and complex experience.

So the features of 'smallness', 'weakness' and 'curiosity', for example, that I work with are not to be divorced from the broader web of childlikeness, even as I self-consciously acknowledge that this inevitably involves some selection, just as 'adult' metaphors are also selective. Selection in itself is not automatically a problem, if acknowledged and if rooted in and placed within a richer context. What if such selection, identifying congruence between certain characteristics of children and the divine nature, is seen to 'idealize' the whole of children's experiences or natures? This argument does not necessarily follow; the congruence is possible without imagining that all children's natures and experiences are intrinsically divine or even good. After all, when we connect adult characteristics with divine nature, we do not suppose that we are viewing all adult life as good. In fact, as I hoped to show in Chapter 2 at least, the childlikeness of God is uncomfortable; it highlights divine solidarity with sites of smallness or belittlement, the hidden cracks of the cosmos where pain and struggle are rife. Such selection, therefore, affirms that childlikeness offers important themes for reflecting on God – and on God's commitments. This is relevant to TOC, and TOC is relevant to the argument, since the reality of children's experience speaks into the solidarity of God's commitments. Even so, I acknowledge that my particular vision of childlikeness or childness can seem quite abstracted – but what I intend is that my starting point is seen as necessarily ambiguous: it is actually a to-and-fro between assumptions about God and assumptions about children, where the two engage in an interplay, as metaphors should. For I do not neatly begin with assumptions about God, projected back on to childness, but nor do I neatly begin with children; instead, the adultness of the divine is interrogated while simultaneously calling the colonial matrix of adult power into question. This is how God's alternative (anti-)empire works: unpicking God-talk and political systems – which is the dual focus of God the Child.

As for CTM, Stollar affirms so much of what it gives, but highlights that its own founders do not regard 'the child in the midst' as centring the experience of children *in themselves*. Rather, as Keith White and Haddon Willmer suggest, the child becomes a symbol of, even a cipher for, other things; so children are not theological agents but, in Stollar's terms, a 'place mat' for particular ideas about God and mission that they want to prioritize.[3] In fact, they are explicit that to regard the centring of the child *as being about children* would be to decentre Jesus and thereby risk idolatry.[4] For them, 'the child is like the mountain' where God is encountered, but it is God, not the mountain, that really matters. They are even, as Stollar notes, more worried about the risk of idolatry than the risk of minimizing children's experience. As such, for my purposes, there is a counter-risk that they miss or downplay the truly subversive revelation of God's solidarity with childness.

For Stollar, Child *Liberation* Theology (CLT), on the other hand, regards the centring of children as intrinsically significant in itself, since children are both theological agents and seekers of liberation – not mere symbols of other matters.[5] It is a distinction between 'the child' as an abstract entity, in CTM, and 'the child' as real experience, in CLT, focused on the injustice endured by children.[6] This distinction is crucial and it raises the question of how my argument for God the Child is located within it. After all, to an extent, 'the child' is abstracted as a selection of certain traits and qualities (smallness, weakness, adventurousness, imaginativeness, curiosity), so it can seem as though I lean towards CTM; but I see it differently. Notably, because of its fear of idolizing the child, CTM stops short of a thorough envisaging of God *as Child*; it sees the childness of God as being dependent on the incarnation, but not that 'the mountain' of encounter with God is actually a 'mole hill', a site of smallness that sheds light on the perpetual childlike-ness of the divine encounter. This limitation means that it does not fully address the particularity of struggle and liberation that is embodied in the experience of little ones, epitomized by children.

In other words, as I was trying to explain above (in Chapters 3 then 4), the focus on God the Child is political – as are affirmations of the Blackness of God, the Disabled God, the Queer God, which Janet Pais also notes.[7] Stollar uses the ana-logy of placing a Black person in the midst of White people and argues that CTM would see this merely as a cipher for talking about God, whereas CLT would see it as political commitment to Black people.[8] I argue that it is both: the political struggle and the theological judgement need and feed each other. A Black God is in solidarity with anti-racist struggle, as we saw in Chapter 3; so too God the Child is in solidarity with the struggle for liberation in the midst of the colonial matrix of adult power.

CLT therefore helps me to make the case more directly: the child in the midst is not another abstract way of talking about God, but a theopolitical way of talking about children. That is to say, the recovery of the centring of children is a theological and political enterprise, inseparable from the childness of God and the critique of the colonial matrix of adult power. That said, I acknowledge my focus is not the liberation of children per se, but how the childness of God makes connections among the range of liberation movements, building solidarity on the grace of the open palm, and developing it here in terms of the disruptiveness of divine agency. In this regard, playfulness is especially potent.

Playfulness

There is a danger in leaping from the theopolitical heart of the argument, with all the realities of injustice borne by children, to the question of playfulness. It can seem like a frivolous leap. It can seem indifferent to the harsh struggles, the domestic abuse, the violence, the neglect, the hunger, the voicelessness, the lack of agency – all of it endured by little ones, notably children as children. How can playfulness not be seen as a way of avoiding those realities? How can it do anything except lift our gaze above the brutalities, as we adults conjure up images of carefree abandon and children lost joyfully in the innocent activity of play?

Such an image, though, would be a seriously misleading interpretation of play. Play, after all, is a serious business.[9] As argued elsewhere, play is an exercise through which people process serious realities – using fantasy or make-believe to work through the struggles, pain, questions and longings of daily life.[10] But play is also not always joyful, or fun – but can be specifically an experience of manipulation, where those with power 'play' with their human pawns; so we should not always rush to an apolitical understanding of it. Play can be deeply political – and unsettling.

Even 'fun' games can be illustrative of the harm done by the 'adult games' we play together; for instance, Monopoly is not merely a lengthy board game concerned with buying properties and collecting rent, but illuminates how capitalism is inclined towards monopolies and how those with wealth accumulate more. We play games with one another, not only as children, but as adults – so to dismiss play as frivolous child play is to distract others, and ourselves, from the much more complex 'power-play' of relationships, habits, norms and structures that justify and exacerbate vested interests, according to the rules of the game set by those with power, while keeping others far away from any meaningful ability to change those rules.

In the dominant game governed by adult rules, children are 'simultaneously childlike and adult',[11] as Paulo Freire recognized, in the sense that the system demands of so many that they must play the role of adult, before their time; bearing the burden of this 'double existence'. They have no control over this; they must play this role to survive, as child labourers. In *God's Heart for Children*, a range of global contributors explore the many ways that children are damagingly impacted by the systems and habits controlled by adults – climate change, trafficking, displacement, as well as gender discrimination.[12] As Ivone Gebara argues too, they directly experience evils, on multiple levels, and therefore offer the possibility of adults' learning being more about the reality of evil through attentiveness to children's experience and agency.[13]

In the face of these dimensions of the colonial matrix of adult power, play is a vital tool – first, in exposing the games and, second, in subverting their rules. And it is a helpful way of understanding so many rebels and misfits in their struggles to reform the systems of our world – not least the social campaigners using direct action and civil disobedience to draw attention to the absurdities in the rules we take for granted and to make visible the possibility of alternative horizons. Campaigns, after all, can have a festival atmosphere, where public debate goes hand in hand with face painting, where peaceful resistance is entangled with childlike imagination. This, it seems, is the world inhabited by Jesus: the world where street theatre, such as on Palm Sunday, exposes and mocks the dominant ways of the mighty, while offering a prophetic and subversive alternative. This is evident especially in Matthew's account, in which Jesus is said to ride a colt and the foal of a donkey – two animals simultaneously, surely uncomfortably, even ridiculously, as though to 'send up' the other great procession that entered Jerusalem every Passover season: the Roman military's procession of prowess. For emperors, like military leaders, may purport to be worthy of the greatest respect, but actually the game they play, riddled with lies and distractions, is worthy of deep mockery.

Play is political – but also theopolitical. It shows us the ways of God: exposing the dominating norms of our social structures and messing with them. In particular, this is the mode of chaos-power: not bolstering a notion of order but destabilizing the bulwarks of false order. A butterfly agency that builds solidarity in the face of all sorts of disabling and life-denying forces, through a whole range of activities, some of them 'under the radar' and some of them public; some humble and some bold; some witty and some enraged. Play through protest, play through conscience-raising, play through alternative-building.

It is the play of the prophet puncturing the pretension of the power-hoarders, the play of the wanderer in the wilderness dreaming new realities, the play of the dove brooding over waters of chaos and soaring towards strange horizons.

It is the play of disruption, destabilizing the norms and forces that hold sway, exposing their absurdities and inconsistencies, their asymmetry and abusiveness, to make possible a wholly different game – of justice, wholeness and life.

God the Child plays with us but does not toy with us. God the Child plays *with* us, alongside us, but also prompts us to tweak and upset the dominant rules of the game, not only to think out of the box, but to disintegrate all known boxes; to tear up and pull down, to destroy and overthrow, but also to build and to plant.

It is the play of one who refuses to accept the power of the status quo, who precociously asks 'Why not?' when told that an alternative is not possible, and who scribbles on the wall defiantly.

Come and see!

Degrowth

The most serious 'game' devised and played by adults is the game constituted by the colonial/capitalist matrix, as analysed by a whole range of ecumenical and liberationist theologians.[14] It is a system that Kevin Snyman lays bare: how 'money has the profound capacity to turn our morality into an impersonal arithmetic calculation', the way that unpayable debt is foundational to the economy, and the interconnections between imperialism, economics and White supremacy.[15] But he and I acknowledge how difficult it is to specify alternatives, because our collective imagination is constrained. As Snyman puts it:

It will only be in the act of recognizing, repenting of, resisting and subverting empire that alternatives will emerge. But we dare not tally. Life on this planet may very well depend on our coming out of empire.[16]

However, the imagination gap is huge. As Fredric Jameson said, 'Someone once said that it is easier to imagine the end of the world than to imagine the end of capitalism.'[17] But according to surveys, there are significant cracks in people's confidence in capitalism: in the USA, 51 per cent of people aged 18–29 don't support capitalism; in 2015, 64 per cent of Britons and as high as 74 per cent of Indians, said they believe capitalism is unfair; and in middle- to higher-income countries, 70 per cent of respondents regard over-consumption as putting the planet and society at risk.[18] This level of public dissonance is never acknowledged. Despite the recent experience of a global pandemic in which resources were deployed by governments towards entirely different ends, and to great effect, we continue to live as though change is not really possible, let alone desired.[19]

Nevertheless, there are alternatives that are advocated, such as 'degrowth', which I explain below[20] – but it too begins with analysis of the connections between colonialism, capitalism and ecological catastrophe. For instance, Jason Hickel argues that colonialism was the means by which most of the Global South was integrated into the capitalist economy – and that it was not at all a benign process, with 100 million excess deaths caused in India alone at the height of British rule.[21] In one episode, the colonizers imposed an intentional policy of income deflation, to appropriate resources for their military expansion, causing 3 million deaths by starvation.[22] The story that is told, however, is that capitalism has lifted many out of poverty – but the evidence suggests that, from the sixteenth century, colonial capitalism worsened human welfare, and it was only the rise of radical social movements in the twentieth century, fighting for improvements in welfare, that mitigated the worst effects of capitalism.[23]

Of course, these colonial disparities continue: for example, research shows that the net worth of resources and labour appropriated *from* the Global South *to* the Global North, just between 1990 and 2015, was $242 trillion[24] – and an estimated 16 million deaths as a result of malnutrition *could* have been avoided had the Global South not been subjected to neoliberal policies and structural adjustments of their economies, which prevented them from enabling people to have universal access to good nutrition.[25] Furthermore, colonialism is also integral to ecological damage: it is countries in the Global North that are responsible for 92 per cent of global emissions in excess of the boundaries of planetary fair-shares;[26] and between 1970 and 2017, rich countries were responsible for 74 per cent of the excess use of global resources.[27] The scope of the interconnected ecological crisis is such that, on the one hand, about one million species are at risk of extinction within decades and, on the other, a global increase in temperature of just 1 degree Celsius will cause a 10 per cent drop in cereal crop yield – and we are heading for an increase between 3 and 4 degrees.[28] Poorer harvests obviously have a disproportionate effect on those surviving in subsidence. Not only is the responsibility for these processes asymmetrical, but the impact of them is also profoundly inequitable.[29]

For Marika Rose, it is striking that the more we seem to know about the trajectory of the game we are playing, the less adequate our response appears to be.[30] She suggests that, despite any predilection to save the world, the only real option is to end it – the world as we know it.[31] One way of understanding this hope is in terms of the righteous fury of God the Child, who dreams of an entirely different game but whose presence is minimized and controlled as a pawn in this one. After all, the devastating game of expansion and extraction – the colonial project that not only moves across territory but enters into it and into its peoples, to colonize *them* and to take from them – has been widely and deeply framed in Christian terms, as 'good news'.[32] We cannot separate ourselves and our habits of defending the prevailing system from the story told by our faith, that God made it so – but 'God' (or specifically our notion of God) has become embroiled within it. Essentially, the game of growth, economically and civilizationally, is entangled with the global growth of Christianity.

What if growth itself is the problem? The game of growth is, for much of the Earth, a game of death. How might God the Child speak to this? After all, for Jim Perkinson, Jesus is a 'downsizer', and we see that, through small things, God denounces the arrogance and deadliness of imperial scale.[33] The

Tower of Babel falls. Egyptian military prowess is devastated. The giant Goliath is defeated. The Temple does not remain, one stone on another. God is rarely about scale, even as we make children sing 'My God is So Big'. We are told, however, that there are no alternatives. But is this true? God the Child dares to ask, 'What if ...?' Might we dare to discover God the Child subversively acting under the radar, evoking a different possibility – one that does not accept the need for growth, but instead celebrates degrowth, downsizing, affirmation of the little? While adults like to tell childlike dreamers that when they grow up they will understand how things have to be like this, it is children who tell adults that they are deceiving themselves – first, because it is 'grown-ups' who have been destroying ecosystems and children's futures, so they should not claim to be the wise ones; and, second, as Greta Thunberg declared, it is adult fantasies or 'fairy tales' of never-ending economic growth that are the delusions.[34] Growing up may not be the answer at all; growth would seem to be devastating.

The tragic irony is this: the system is defended as though it is the most rational thing, but by reducing human life to *Homo economicus*[35] and leading us into such self-destructive crises, it shows itself to be riddled with fantastical delusions of unlimited growth.[36] Meanwhile, the seemingly childlike alternatives, which embrace the 'poetry' that life is so much more than the relentless bottom line,[37] are the ones that talk sense. But this does not make children the real grown-ups; rather, childness is integral to such revolutionary insight. We encounter this further in Chapters 7 and 8.

For Hickel, there is another specific irony: that the global economy is built around the notion of growth, even as many richer countries are struggling to grow their economies, but 2–3 per cent growth is needed globally to meet the necessary level of profits.[38] We become locked in this cycle of uncritical belief in growth,[39] while barely achieving it yet still insisting it alone is the means to make a better world. Even 'green growth' is a myth, necessarily harnessing nature 'into circuits of extraction and production' to fulfil goals of growth.[40] Of course, there is plenty of growth, but it is massively directed towards a tiny proportion of the population, the richest 1 per cent taking the gains of a quarter of all economic activity ($19 trillion per year, as of 2020).[41] In other words, financial capitalism plays by its own rules, its figurative currency casinos betting on market slumps,[42] and the elites hoard the fruits while the number of people depending on foodbanks increases – and creation groans. Other stories and other futures are available, however. Hickel argues that degrowth can make so much more sense than the lie of growth-obsession; it can enable us to achieve rapid decarbonization, reduce ecological harm and increase social benefits.[43] As an alternative economic model, it achieves these goals through particular commitments:[44] managing a diversion away from less-necessary production (fossil fuels, mass meat and dairy, fast fashion, cars and aircraft), increasing the lifespan of new products[45] and focusing on public goods (health, education, transport, internet, sustainable energy, nutritious food), which will require different funding models (including taxes on wealth and ecological harm), cancelling of unfair debt on lower-income countries, and the 'greening' of employment.

At its heart, it is not that the goal of degrowth is to shrink the economy; rather, it is to re-create the economy such that there is a shift away from *the need for growth*. It is about becoming post-capitalist, orientating towards different and higher goals – of human and environmental flourishing.[46] Nor is it about working within what environmentalists call 'limits', because instead it refocuses our attention on the interconnectedness of life, affirming nature as gift to which we too must give.[47] As Vincent Liegey and Anitra Nelson put it:

> Degrowth is neither a dogma nor a reductionist concept ... Degrowth is a set of thoughts aimed at shaking people's belief in growthism. In its place, degrowth offers a platform for debates and convergence, for re-appropriating hope through inventing, discussing, experimenting with and implementing democratic and peaceful transitions. Transitions to new models of society based on ... the enjoyment of life, open relocalization, sustainability, frugal abundance, conviviality and autonomy.[48]

Participants in the Research and Degrowth network express it in these terms:

> Degrowth challenges the hegemony of growth and calls for a democratically led redistributive downscaling of production and consumption in industrialized countries as a means to achieve environmental sustainability, social justice and well-being.[49]

They denote its particular location as a movement in the Global North, where responsibility for colonial capitalism and ecological catastrophe dwell. But as a movement for change, its connections extend far and wide, since it is profoundly relevant to, shaped by and vital for the Global South; it cuts across those divides, with global ecological and social justice being paramount.[50] The networks therefore include those seeking reparations, refugees and migrants arguing 'We are here because you destroy our countries', and many more alliances.[51] Flowing from these relationships and practices, there would be many gains. For example, if we reorientate towards public goods (health and education), all social goals for *all* people, globally, can be met with *less* GDP.[52] Also, 'frugal abundance' is about 'letting go of work, consumption and environmentally unfriendly activities to make space and time to enjoy a rich quality of life coextensive with a low ecological footprint'.[53] This further illustrates the connectivity between people, work, leisure, ecology and well-being.

Of course, this seemingly utopian direction of travel will require careful management and international commitments,[54] but Hickel takes encouragement both from existing social movements that understand the importance of well-being and the lessons that can be learned from experimental projects such as 'transition towns', cooperatives and progressive cities.[55] It will necessarily be an adaptable movement, widely inclusive, consciously decolonial (therefore attentive to both class and 'race'[56]), and 'glocally' embedded.[57] The economist Jeremy Rifkin also glimpses an emerging alternative economy, one centred around a 'collaborative commons' of producers and consumers bypassing markets, confronting the 'entropic bill' of climate change and fostering relationships across borders – which are focused on empathy (reviving *Homo empathicus*), and therefore not naïve about suffering but very attentive to it.[58]

In the face of the dominant game, with its seemingly unquestionable rules, this alternative game of degrowth can seem precocious – like a child asserting itself audaciously in a grown-up world. It can sound like a lone and quiet voice, drowned out by the noisy waves of muscular neoliberal capitalism that insists it is the only way. Yet as noted above, the global pandemic showed us that active government in collaboration with public goodwill and solidarity can be harnessed in a profound emergency; but the desired transformations require 'change ... without taking power'.[59] Faced with the same old normal in that governments deny their own capacity for long-term thinking and transformative action, the solution is 'a decentralized and horizontal network of small collectives and projects', turning 'power over' into 'power to' – that is, empowering people to play their part.[60] Elsewhere, I affirm such 'coalitions of chaos',[61] taking an apparently disparaging term and using it positively, to point to the propensity for solidarity movements to stir up questions, 'opening up people's consciousness to the possibility of creating an alternative world'.[62]

This quest for justice may be glimpsed as a child playfully messing up the game that takes its own seriousness for granted; an act of disruption that protests against intransigent and deluded adults and promises a different prospect: a 'smaller' game, stripped of impenetrable economic logic, one that instead enables everyone to play, where even winning takes on a new meaning, in the service of the little people and of the Earth, whose tiniest creatures and stones cry out, whose seas roar with rage and joy and whose mountains and hills clap their hands.

It is a world in which everyone has enough. No one is hungry. Rivers flow, nourishing the trees whose leaves are for the healing of the nations. And children play in the streets.

Hymn: Creation groans

This is inspired by the activism and words of Greta Thunberg, in particular her 'How dare you!' speech to the UN Climate Action Summit, 23 September 2019, where she said, 'We are in the beginning of a mass extinction and all you can talk about is money and fairytales of eternal economic growth.'

Creation groans, a girl skips school,
a movement swells, their voices join:
'How dare you steal our future life
while other interests take your coin?'

We've hurt our home, its ice caps melt,
the oceans swell while forests burn.
How dare we hide in fairy tales
of constant growth and fail to learn.

We need to dream, but wide awake
to face the painful truth we've known:
the Earth laments as millions move
and reap a crisis we have sown.

My mind and eyes will spring with tears;
my faith, though just a mustard seed,
will join with yours to move this mount;
'this world is God's' my guiding creed.

(Graham Adams, 2020)
Suggested tune: *Rockingham*

Questions

1 Do you see the political nature of God the Child on the side of those who are belittled in our world and transforming our complacently adult images of God, in order to celebrate the childlike dream of a more just world?

2 How about playfulness as political – in particular, disrupting the rules of dominant games, to make way for new rules, new games, new possibilities?

3 What do you make of degrowth – both as an alternative economic model and as a theological commitment, downsizing in the face of obsessions with scale and grandeur?

Notes

1 I noted in Chapter 4 that I had used this term previously in: Graham Adams, 2024 (forthcoming), 'Mission in the Colonial Matrix of Adult Power: Child-centredness as Way, Truth, Life!', in Benjamin Aldous, Harvey Kwiyani, Peniel Rajkumar and Victoria Turner (eds), *'Lived' Mission in 21st Century Britain: Ecumenical and Postcolonial Perspectives*, London: SCM Press.

2 R. L. Stollar, 2016, 'Using vs Liberating Children: How Child Theology Differs from Child Liberation Theology', 26 April, https://rlstollar.com/2016/04/26/using-vs-liberating-children-how-child-theology-differs-from-child-liberation-theology/?amp=1 (accessed 16.7.23).

3 Stollar, 'Using vs Liberating Children'; and Keith J. White and Haddon Willmer, *An Introduction to Child Theology*, London: The Child Theology Movement Limited, p. 6, https://childtheologymovement.org/wp-content/uploads/2020/11/Booklet-1-Intro-to-Child-Theology-sample.pdf (accessed 07.12.23).

4 White and Willmer, *An Introduction to Child Theology*, pp. 6–7.

5 Rohan P. Gideon also engages with the question of children's agency in the context of their vulnerabilities: 'Soteriology and Children's Vulnerabilities and Agency', in Marcia J. Bunge (ed.), 2021, *Child Theology: Diverse Methods and Global Perspectives*, Maryknoll, NY: Orbis, pp. 90ff.

6 See, coming out of an Ecuadorian context, Maria Alejandra Andrade Vinueza, 2022, 'Spirituality and Hope: The Extraordinary Hidden within the Ordinary', in Rosalind Tan, Nativity A. Petallar and Lucy A. Hefford (eds), *God's Heart for Children: Practical Theology from Global Perspectives*, Carlisle: Langham Publishing, p. 129: how children manage to continue hoping, to survive, in the midst of desperate circumstances. Similarly, in South Africa, see Dirk J. Smit, 2021, 'Reimagining Hope *with* and *like* Children', in Bunge (ed.), *Child Theology*, pp. 209ff.

7 Janet Pais, 1991, *Suffer the Children: A Theology of Liberation by a Victim of Child Abuse*, Mahwah, NJ: Paulist Press, p. 15.

8 Stollar, 'Using vs Liberating Children', Conclusion.

9 As noted also in Chapter 2: Brian Edgar, 2017, *The God Who Plays: A Playful Approach to Theology and Spirituality*, Eugene, OR: Cascade Books, p. 1.

10 David Hay and Rebecca Nye, 2006, *The Spirit of the Child*, rev. edn, London and Philadelphia: Jessica Kingsley Publishers, pp. 73–4; Edgar, *The God Who Plays*, p. 45 (play as relationship-developing); Graham Adams, 2022, *Holy Anarchy: Dismantling Domination, Embodying Community, Loving Strangeness*, London: SCM Press, p. 167.

11 Walter Omar Kohan, 2021, *Paulo Freire: A Philosophical Biography*, London: Bloomsbury, p. 127.

12 Tan, Petallar and Hefford (eds), *God's Heart for Children*.

13 Ivone Gebara, 2021, 'Children's Experiences of Evil in their Multiple Worlds', in Bunge (ed.), *Child Theology*, pp. 52ff.

14 Adams, *Holy Anarchy*, pp. 73–80.

15 Kevin Snyman, 2023, '"Come We Go Chant Down Babylon": How Black Liberation Theology Subverts White Privilege and Dismantles the Economics of Empire to Save the Planet', in Anthony G. Reddie and Carol Troupe (eds), *Deconstructing Whiteness, Empire and Mission*, London: SCM Press, pp. 266, 267, 268ff. See also Kehinde Andrews, 2021, *The New Age of Empire: How Racism and Colonialism Still Rule the World*, London: Penguin.

16 Snyman, '"Come We Go Chant"', p. 276.

17 Fredric Jameson, 2006, 'First Impressions', *London Review of Books*, 27(17), 7 September, cited by Marika Rose, 2023, *Theology for the End of the World*, London: SCM Press, p. 4; and Jason Hickel, 2020, *Less is More: How Degrowth Will Save the World*, London: Penguin, p. 24.

18 Hickel, *Less is More*, pp. 24–6.

19 Tim Jackson, 2021, *Post Growth: Life after Capitalism*, Cambridge: Polity Press, p. 148.

20 See also Vincent Liegey and Anitra Nelson, 2020, *Exploring Degrowth: A Critical Guide*, London: Pluto Press; Jackson, *Post

Growth; and Matthias Schmelzer, Andrea Vetter and Aaron Vansintjan, 2022, *The Future is Degrowth: A Guide to a World beyond Capitalism*, London and New York: Verso.

21 Dylan Sullivan and Jason Hickel, 2022, 'How British Colonialism Killed 100 Million Indians in 40 years', *Al Jazeera*, 2 December, https://t.co/hPU2QfvFX2 (accessed 07.12.23).

22 Jason Hickel, 2022, 'How British Colonizers Caused the Bengal Famine', *New Internationalist*, 21 January, https://t.co/YCoA6kbJgW (accessed 30.7.23).

23 Dylan Sullivan and Jason Hickel, 2023, 'Capitalism and Extreme Poverty: A Global Analysis of Real Wages, Human Height, and Mortality since the Long 16th Century', *ScienceDirect: World Development*, 161, January, https://t.co/5VeqzmZNkX (accessed 07.12.23).

24 Jason Hickel et al., 2022, 'Imperialist Appropriation in the World Economy: Drain from the Global South through Unequal Exchange 1990–2015', *ScienceDirect: Global Environmental Change*, 73, March, https://t.co/FWDS4jVroe (accessed 30.7.23). See also Schmelzer, Vetter and Vansintjan, *The Future is Degrowth*, pp. 157, 291.

25 Dylan Sullivan and Jason Hickel, 2022, '16 Million and Counting: The Collateral Damage of Capital', *New Internationalist*, 22 December, https://t.co/WGJd5gSJ78 (accessed 30.7.23).

26 Jason Hickel, 2022, 'Who is Responsible for Climate Breakdown?', *Al Jazeera*, 4 April, https://t.co/uUn47ff1Jr (accessed 30.7.23).

27 Jason Hickel et al., 2022, 'National Responsibility for Ecological Breakdown: A Fair-shares Assessment of Resource-use, 1970–2017', *The Lancet: Planetary Health*, 6(4), April, e342–e349, https://t.co/OUT8aS9iE0 (accessed 30.07.23).

28 Hickel, *Less is More*, pp. 9, 13.

29 Hickel, *Less is More*, p. 21.

30 Rose, *Theology for the End of the World*, p. 2.

31 Rose, *Theology for the End of the World*, p. 10.

32 See, for instance, Kenneth Leech, *Struggle in Babylon: Racism in the Cities and the Churches of Britain*, London: Sheldon Press, 1988; Robert Beckford, 2020, *Dread and Pentecostal: A Political Theology for the Black Church in Britain*, London: SPCK; and Anthony G. Reddie, 2019, *Theologizing Brexit: A Liberationist and Postcolonial Critique*, London and New York: Taylor & Francis, p. 25: how 'Mission Christianity' shaped White supremacy and Black self-negation. David Clough discusses these and other connected dynamics in society, between the state, monarchy and aristocracy, class and church, each fuelling entrenched privileges: 2023, 'Deconstructing Whiteness in the UK Christian Theological Academy', in Reddie and Troupe (eds), *Deconstructing Whiteness*, p. 33.

33 James W. Perkinson, 2021, 'Coronavirus Cacophony: When the

Dwarf Rebukes the Giant', in Jione Havea (ed.), in *Doing Theology in the New Normal: Global Perspectives*, London: SCM Press, p. 228.

34 Greta Thunberg, 2019, 'How Dare You!', speech to the UN Climate Action Summit, 23 September, https://www.npr.org/2019/09/23/763452863/transcript-greta-thunbergs-speech-at-the-u-n-climate-action-summit (accessed 31.7.23) – 'You are still not mature enough to tell it like it is!'

35 See Liegey and Nelson, 2022, *Exploring Degrowth*, p. 46; and Cynthia D. Moe-Lobeda, 2002, *Healing a Broken World: Globalization and God*, Minneapolis, MN: Augsburg Fortress, pp. 110–11.

36 Néstor Míguez, Joerg Rieger and Jung Mo Sung, 2009, *Beyond the Spirit of Empire*, London: SCM Press, p. 130; also Jung Mo Sung, 2007, *Desire, Market and Religion*, London: SCM Press, p. 21.

37 See, for example, Jackson, *Post Growth*, p. 180.

38 Hickel, *Less is More*, p. 20.

39 Moe-Lobeda, *Healing a Broken World*, pp. 110–11.

40 Hickel, *Less is More*, pp. 23, 139ff.

41 Hickel, *Less is More*, p. 29, citing the World Inequality Database.

42 Jackson, *Post Growth*, p. 138, speaks of 'the casino economy'. As told by the book and film *The Big Short*, individuals can make millions by betting on a recession or market crash – for example, see https://www.historic-cornwall.org.uk/how-much-did-cornwall-capital-make-the-big-short/ (accessed 30.7.23).

43 Hickel, 2022, 'Degrowth Can Work – Here's How Science Can Help', *Nature*, 12 December, https://nature.com/articles/d41586-022-04412-x (accessed 30.7.23).

44 Hickel, 'Degrowth Can Work'.

45 See Hickel, *Less is More*, pp. 209–12.

46 Hickel, *Less is More*, pp. 30–1.

47 Hickel, *Less is More*, p. 34.

48 Liegey and Nelson, *Exploring Degrowth*, p. 48.

49 Federico Demaria et al., 2013, 'What is Degrowth? From an Activist Slogan to a Social Movement', *Environmental Values*, 22(2), p. 209.

50 Schmelzer, Vetter and Vansintjan, *The Future is Degrowth*, pp. 194–5.

51 Schmelzer, Vetter and Vansintjan, *The Future is Degrowth*, p. 245, citing Olaf Bernau, 2020, 'Refugee Movement: Struggling with Migration and Escape', in Corinna Burkhart, Matthias Schmelzer and Nina Treu (eds), *Degrowth in Movement(s): Exploring Pathways for Transformation*, Winchester: Zero Books, pp. 272–86.

52 Hickel, *Less is More*, p. 178.

53 Liegey and Nelson, *Exploring Degrowth*, p. 61.

54 Schmelzer, Vetter and Vansintjan, *The Future is Degrowth*, pp. 244ff.

55 See Hickel, 'Degrowth Can Work'.

56 Schmelzer, Vetter and Vansintjan, *The Future is Degrowth*, p. 289.

57 Liegey and Nelson, *Exploring Degrowth*, p. 131.

58 Jeremy Rifkin, 2014, *The Zero Marginal Cost Society: The Internet of Things, the Collaborative Commons and the Eclipse of Capitalism*, New York: Palgrave Macmillan, pp. 10, 11, 14, 16f., 183–92, 301.

59 Liegey and Nelson, *Exploring Degrowth*, p. 89.

60 Liegey and Nelson, *Exploring Degrowth*, p. 90.

61 Graham Adams, 2023, 'Holy Anarchy as an Alternative Ecology of Living Possibilities', in Kevin Snyman and Lawrence Heath-Moore (eds), *Revolting Christians: Theologies in Action*, Manchester: Walking the Way Publications, p. 7.

62 Liegey and Nelson, *Exploring Degrowth*, p. 93.

6

The Dis/ability of the Agency

*'If any of you put a stumbling-block before one of these
little ones who believe in me, it would be better for you
if a great millstone were hung around your neck and you
were thrown into the sea.'*
(Mark 9.42)

Obstacles and prayer

To pursue God's new world, we must face obstacles: systems,
habits and attitudes that impede the flourishing of life. God the
Child shows the way, bending through the cracks in the walls,
humming and dancing to made-up tunes of hopefulness, while
also playfully processing the pain and struggle of life. Not indifferent to the trauma, not naively distant from it, but telling
stories, finding new symbols, sitting in silence, pointing to the
horizon, an arm around those who weep, an inner rage in the
face of cruelty and catastrophe, a tearful determination. But
even then, the obstacles can be too great, and the children with
whom God the Child sings in solidarity are themselves victims
of these systems, bearing the broken dreams of a world reck-
less with their own future. The vision is of a new world where
children lead the way, their attentiveness to the tiniest creature
and their wonder at the vast sky teaching us empathy and imagination, but they are the very ones shut out, kept down,
excluded from the feast and neglected. Jesus warns us against
such idiocy, but still we allow these habits to prosper, in social
life and religion – where children are patronized or silenced, not
seen as the very foundation of creation's renewal.[1]

On the way towards better habits, may we learn to pray, at
least, and allow the prayer to inhabit our dreams and practice:

God, our heavenly Child,
May you be praised in all creation!
May your imaginative scribbles of a new world come into
being,
May your dreams and visions be fulfilled on earth.
May we give and receive, inspired by your open hand, until
everyone has what they need.
May we change our minds, learn and forgive, as you show
us how to let go.
May you fly a kite that guides us, caught up in the breath of
hope, towards better horizons.
May you show us how to rage against what is unfair and
cruel, until these things crumble.
For your chaos-power, your glorious imagination and your
wonder-full dream of new creation fill us with hope and
determination,
Now and always,
Amen

Dis/ability?

As I have tried to show, our understanding of God is closely
tied up with our experience of structures that work against the
full dignity, inclusion and participation of all. In terms of God
as Child, our appreciation of or resistance to it is intimately
interwoven with our own particular awareness or unawareness
of structures that obstruct children, or little ones of any kind. If
we do not see the effects of prevailing patterns, and perhaps we
even defend them, we may be less likely to allow for the reality of God as Child, with potentially profound consequences.
But if we recognize how these patterns work and who suffers
because of them, we begin to make room for alternative models
of God, wriggling restlessly in the corners and cracks. Or to
put it another way, if we find these models compelling in some
respects, we may also find ourselves seeing how adult-centred
structures leave little room for little ones.

The adult-centred structures consist of what I called, in

Chapter 4, 'the colonial matrix of adult power': the system that frames expectations, but also imagination. It delimits how we can conceive not only relationships between different people, but also the very notion and nature of God.

But we might ask: Why does God simply not undermine this matrix and its power? Why does God not just get on with dismantling it, leaving us to see reality more straightforwardly and to see the fullness of divine nature? The usual answer to that, which Christians reach for, is the necessity of our freedom: God leaves things a certain way because our freedom matters deeply to God. But there is another answer, more closely related to the nature of divine power: while our freedom matters hugely, freedom in itself is not so straightforward; rather, the issue here is God's 'chaos-power', which is not the sort of capacity that can impose its will but nevertheless elicits or effects potential consequences.

In other words, there is a certain 'disability' when it comes to divine power. But notions of disability must be handled with care. In particular, disabled people have often been patronized as childlike, so I must be as explicit as possible, as in relation to Blackness and childness too: I am not saying that these experiences are the same, but rather that they can be allies with each other, each challenging systems that belittle, marginalize and oppress. Disability and childness are experiences that both understand what it means to be subjected to a colonial matrix of power – and can expose it and subvert it. They also offer important insights into the nature of God and God's power, as the basis for such exposure and subversion. It is, in fact, the 'disabled God' and the 'childlike God' who, as with the Black God or the Queer God, represent push-back against prevailing assumptions, habits and structures, if not outright but subtle rebellion in the face of them. This does not mean a 'disabled' God is the same as saying that God is 'childlike'; rather, they each add to the other, as subversive contributions to a more comprehensive undoing of dominant theopolitical dynamics.

However, my previous excursions into Disability theology have been limited and one-sided.[2] To a certain extent, it is difficult to avoid this because we are always coming from somewhere, in some ways recognizing this and in other ways not fully appreciating the implications of our particular location or story. And, of course, it is a dynamic area of theology, in which terminology and ideas slip through our fingers even as we think we grasp them. Nevertheless, I recognize that I stumbled my way into it, well-intentioned but without quite fully naming my location. After all, my particular experience was crucial, my mum having lived with disability since I was eight years old, very much shaping how I engaged with the world and informing my theological interests, even when they weren't directly addressing matters of disability. They had caused me to seek out justice, paying attention to those not noticed or heeded, on a range of fronts – but I had not pursued these things in the context of disability directly. When I did so, I realize that I came to it as an ally of disabled people but not sufficiently attentive to a complexity within Disability theologies – which is how many of us come to give support to others. By owning here a particular limitation in my contribution, I hope this will further illuminate the way God's disabled power must be addressed with care.

The thing was, I insisted that I wanted to put personhood before disability, so I would speak of 'people with disabilities' rather than 'disabled people' – and this was clearly affected by my relationship with my mum; to me, she was Mum, a person in relationship, prior to the question of her disability. She was deeply capable in a wide range of capacities, even as she was also impeded in many ways. So I have found it helpful to speak of 'dis/ability', not wrenching the two realities apart, because they are indeed intertwined, but sensing that disability is not the whole of the person's identity. On the basis of this personal experience, I wanted to affirm some general commitments – about the importance of the person coming first, including with their respective 'abilities', putting the 'dis' in some degree of context. But I failed to address the complexity of that context more fully, since it is not the whole truth to say personhood precedes condition. The social model of disability clarifies that people do not merely 'have' a disability, like an appendage they carry around; rather, the very structures of society in which they move 'disable' them. The 'conditions' in question are not simply bodily and medical, but are systemic and societal. In other words, people are 'disabled' by the matrix of power; they are 'disabled people', their very personhood shaped in the context of systems and forces outside their control. To name the reality as such is an important step towards addressing it. Yes, it would be wonderful if people could be, simply, people with disabilities, but structures work against this aspiration: they are disabled people.

Of course, though, both things can be true together. But I wanted to emphasize how my location in the discussion had caused me to incline towards one term rather than the other. In effect, I had downplayed the social model of disability (which identifies how people are 'disabled' by society), out of loyalty to my mum (whose personhood I sought to affirm *in itself*). Our location matters, for good and for ill. We see some things, we overlook others. As a result, we need other voices to help us see the picture more fully. Miriam Spies, for instance, notes that able-bodied people can be quick to look for what can be affirmed, in the experiences of disability, whereas disabled people themselves need to be heard on their terms, for all the discomfort that this may bring to able-bodied sensibilities.[3] The reality for many disabled people, after all, is existential struggle. It is the open-handedness of God that receives the complexity of these different experiences, including the awkwardness.

So it is with debates about divine power and agency. Our location is important. It is very tempting for me, for various reasons, to argue that God does not have the sort of power to overturn certain features of our world; that God is in fact 'disabled' in contrast with our desires for divine capacity – but I can appreciate that others, perhaps those in far more desperate situations than me, need to affirm God's ability to defeat forces of evil and bring clear liberation. Location affects theology. It is easy to say 'God is disabled', but the implications of this are partly unknown – at least in the sense that I cannot know exactly how it is received by others. But I also recognize that others, including those in or alongside situations of deep struggle, do indeed challenge the expectation that God will sort things out. Miguel de La Torre insists that 'hopelessness' must have its rightful place, as we discussed previously in Chapter 2: it is a necessary corrective to the optimistic expectation of divine intervention, since such optimism may discourage us from engaging in action ourselves. If we wait for God to intervene, we may be assuming that all God expects of us is patience; whereas God may be calling forth an active solidarity to challenge and uproot the systems of injustice – and it may only be a due regard for 'hopelessness' that sparks this defiance in us.

It is not that an 'able God' will ride roughshod over our disabled will and agency, but that a disabled God will spark activity, ability and agency among us, in solidarity with one another. For Nancy Eiesland, the disability of God affirms that God is a 'survivor', in solidarity with those who are also survivors in the midst of structural obstacles[4] – and affirms God's 'interdependence' with us, as opposed to solely independent of our own agency or indeed solely dependent on us.[5] Lisa Powell argues for a disabled God who 'stakes God's own being on relationship with creation, on the frailty of the human form, on the gift-giving of those with whom God covenants'.[6] In my terms, the disabled agency of the childlike God, in their awesome weakness, will evoke and work with the disabled agencies of others.

On the one hand, the implication of this could be that 'disability' renders an agent capable of playing only the smallest part, the fluttering of a butterfly's fragile wing, unable to ensure a hurricane of transformation comes, but nevertheless generating the possibility of it, through such awesome weakness. On the other hand, disabled people combined with disabled people and, as appropriate, with able-bodied people, and childlikeness allying with adulthood, can be a much stronger force than a 'mere' fluttering wing; it is a movement of solidarity, chaining metaphorical wheelchairs to figurative fences, capable of transforming social practices and structures, through protest, campaigning, organizing and elements of revolt. God's dis/abled agency may be like this too – the basis for and enabler of the deepest and broadest possible 'interdependence'.

Does this mean that God's power is 'disabled' in the sense of the social model – that is, disabled by the colonial matrix of adult power? Or is God's power disabled by its intrinsic incapacity to act in a certain brute way? This question highlights an issue: is God's nature and power the sort of agency that exists in and of itself, separate from any entanglements with wider social life? I do not think that it is, which means that the choice between 'social model disability' and 'medical disability', in relation to divine power, is a false dichotomy. It is *both* true that God intrinsically cannot act in a brute way (rather, God's agency is always limited to chaos-power, the awesome weakness of the fluttering wing or childlike agency) *and* that God's effectiveness is itself affected by the structures that social life inhabits. This complexity, which is reflected in our own human embodiment, is also true of God. At the same time, the disabled agency of humans and God can build solidarities of effective agency; even though our powers seem 'merely' childlike, the coalition of chaos-events can be a force of considerable impact. For Lisa Powell, 'God relies upon the creature not only for the completion of God's plan, but also for the fulfilment of the divine life itself.'[7]

Such divine agency is, therefore, an agency that comes up against structures of resistance, unable to overthrow them straightforwardly.

It is an agency that is itself 'disabled' in contrast with certain adult-shaped perceptions, which are conditioned by able-bodiedness; it is unable to guarantee its will is done, but nevertheless it generates possibilities. Powell locates this in the context of 'covenant ontology', an approach to God that 'positions God as vulnerable, since God risks the "fulfilment" or "completion" of [anticipated] divine life in the humanity of Jesus'; in this way, God is not 'self-sufficient' at all, so 'undercutting the very social elevation of independence as a virtue'.[8] I continue to work with Powell's ideas below, much as I conversed with Karen O'Donnell's in Chapter 2, because they engage with key issues for my purposes and they are recent.

The agency of God the Child, fostered in this way, is an agency that is dis/abled but can be combined with other dis/abled agents, in pursuit of transformations that might not yet be imagined.

Ambiguities

The image of the disabled *child* helps to make the point all the more poignantly. Here we see that, although disability and childness are not synonymous, they certainly can and do inhabit the same life – a disabled child – which is true not only of some people, but may be true of the divine life as well. For this is not God the Parent, caring for us in our incapacity. Indeed, the child is often the one who cares for the parent in any case; child carers of adults being widespread, and sometimes briefly lauded, but certainly not fully recognized or supported. Instead, God may be the one in whom we see complex and multiple disabilities, evoking our care, attentiveness, love; perhaps one who cannot articulate their exact needs, except through a sequence of blinks or sounds that we must lovingly learn to interpret appropriately; or who struggles and manages to overcome certain obstacles while being 'defeated' by many others – and one who may show us an uncomplicated love, a beautiful love, a disabled love. Again, Eiesland captures these tensions in terms of the 'mixed blessing' of disability, taking seriously the despair while also acknowledging how insights and gifts arise that otherwise might not.[9]

Powell, too, affirms God's vulnerability and need. For her, it centres on the 'receptivity' of God; that is, in order to fulfil God's covenantal purposes, God 'needs' to receive from the human and, in Jesus, God thereby empties their self in order to receive humanity.[10] There are different views as to the *risk* of such receptivity: for Bruce McCormack, it is not as risky as it seems, because God's 'extensive foreknowledge' knows how Jesus will fulfil God's anticipation;[11] but for Paul Dafydd Jones, there is real risk.[12] Interestingly, Powell says that in hindsight 'we see victory as assured', but that 'this does not alter the risk in the real history of Jesus' lifetime'[13] – so underscoring the significance of divine risk, an essentially relational way of being; it is in effect throwing oneself on to the grace and responsiveness of others. Personally, however, I would not speak of victory as assured, even with hindsight, because I see the cross-turned-resurrection 'victory' of God the Child as necessarily more ambiguous: it is, after all, capable of being, on the one hand, seen as a failure (since widespread transformation flowing from it is not easy to discern) and, on the other, misused as a brute-force victory (whereby the church takes sides with crucifiers, to justify other kinds of violence as divinely ordained); therefore some acknowledgement of the ambiguity and ambivalence of the 'disabled victory', as a chaos-event, may be helpful. Nevertheless, the point of Powell's discussion is helpfully to highlight how God's covenant ontology – that is, God's commitment to foster relationship and participation – entails genuine risk and vulnerability on God's part. This is 'promising' for Disability theology, because in God's own disability God must risk relying on the fragile agency of human life, not only of Jesus' life but Mary's[14] and others'; that is, we too are invited into this disabled embodiment of God's purposes.

To see the interplay between God's acts and ours in these terms is to affirm God's 'posture of openness to the gift of the other', a 'productive power in intimacy', which is therefore not a receptivity of 'passivity' but a receptivity of agency: it is a will to relatedness, rather than maintaining a hierarchy or binary of one agent and the other.[15] In other words, as subtle and messy as it may seem, the disabled God does not only receive, but gives, and does not only give, but also receives.[16] For Powell, 'the receptivity of the Son [as she locates this specifically in the Son] signals the eternal value of interdependence and life intertwined in care, reception of care, and assistance in care.'[17]

Powell incisively engages also with the intersections between gender and disability, in particular in the context of 'kenotic christology';[18] that is, those understandings of Christ that argue that God has self-emptied in becoming human. She sketches the feminist critiques of kenotic models: first, they leave us with a vulnerable Christ, which in itself is problematic because, when projected on to women, it can romanticize their vulnerability, whereas what they need is agency, autonomy, strength; and, second, the model can feed gender stereotypes of male agency and female passivity, even where *Christ's* vulnerability is being centred – because it is seen as a feminization of God. Disability theologians respond that these critiques avoid disabled experience (the sheer reality of vulnerability, dependency, non-autonomy), so further marginalizing disabled people's stories and agency.[19] Also, in light of Marcella Althaus-Reid's Queer theology (to which we return in Chapter 9), there is a sense in which feminists are wary of 'uncontrolled bodies',[20] both those not enacting their own autonomy and, in effect, disabled bodies whose movements are beyond control. Sarah Coakley's solution is to affirm kenosis as 'space-making';[21] that is, God makes room for the other – which is what my image of the open hand signifies. But I agree with Powell that, while Coakley affirms space-making, she unhelpfully rejects divine vulnerability – whereas a disabled God embraces it.[22] My issue with kenotic Christology, after all, is not that a certain sort of power was 'given up', but that it was regarded as existing within God in the first place, as I note also in Chapter 7.

Finally, for my purposes, Powell's discussion of the dynamics between both divine and human giving and receiving, as helpful as it is for illuminating gendered assumptions, nevertheless takes for granted that all such dynamics occur in an *adult* framework. In particular, she analyses how what is, in effect, the heteropatriarchal matrix of power identifies a hierarchy within Christ: it contrasts the divine agency, which is viewed as active and male, with human receptivity, seen as passive and female. In such a gendered hierarchy/binary, the metaphors are also sexual, since the divine agency 'penetrates' human receptivity.[23] This is clearly adult – with no appropriate space-making for the child. Powell qualifies it with reference to what is called 'queer crip Christology', which destabilizes the binary both from a queer perspective and in the light of disability. She proceeds to reconfigure the dynamics, between divine and human, on the basis of 'queer crip sex'.[24] While this is valuable within the unexamined adult nature of the matrix of power, an entirely different approach is needed vis-à-vis God the Child. I have argued elsewhere that Christ need not and should not always be seen as the divine initiator, rather as one receiving others' agency;[25] it is what I call 'social christology', Christ's very identity being bound up with others' identities in a dynamic of 'mutual humanization'.[26] This does not imply sexualized images at all; in fact, it aligns well with the proverb 'It takes a village to raise a child'. So with God the Child: the divine agency is both active/assertive and receptive, both energetic and learning, both an open hand and a chaos-event. God the Child, as disabled, is both vulnerable and a survivor; giver of joy and dependent on others; unable to control their body and nevertheless able to evoke responses in others and to enjoy those responses.

By acknowledging the disability of God, in connection with God as Child, I am not seeking to idealize or romanticize these realities, as though it is a way of 'rescuing' genuine physical struggles through affirming their likeness with divine agency. It is not at all to pretend that these things can simply transcend their reality, minimizing the pain, the heartache and the way such traumas reconfigure people's dreams and aspirations. Rather, it is to affirm how God speaks and acts: not through the direct lines of adult articulacy, or able-bodied precision, but the meaningful murmurs, cues and chaos-events of intent, hope, anticipation, fragile but determined action – no matter how disabled they are. Intersecting with these tensions, Claire Williams identifies how, in the context of motherhood and *autism*, the narrative of 'autism as a tragedy' meets the model of neurodiversity – the pain meets the potential for celebration – and to handle the tensions, whether between affirmation and struggle, or our similarities and differences, she highlights the significance of 'solidarity': a determination to be alongside one another.[27] Indeed, these experiences are not 'the same' as disability, but the tensions nevertheless bear some similarities.

God is like a disabled child precisely because it makes no more sense to view God as an able-bodied adult. The metaphorical force of the former is that it goes some way to resolving the questions rightly raised in light of the latter – questions about God's relationship with suffering, struggle, injustice. It reminds us how any such modelling is metaphor, or analogy. It highlights that there will always be constructive ambiguity in the different dimensions of religious purpose: the pursuit of truth, beauty and goodness. In other words, there is a necessary ambiguity about the *truth* of the divine nature, and agency, because without such ambiguity the human giants who purport to grasp the truth would wield their power unaccountably; whereas the ambiguity of the metaphors helps to humble their pretensions. There is a necessary ambiguity over its beauty, otherwise people would insist that beauty can only be seen in a certain way, whereas it can be present and real in all kinds of 'disabled' contexts. And there is a necessary ambiguity over its goodness, not just in the sense that how we conceive of goodness may be evil and vice versa – but it is our ambiguous grasp of one another's personhood that helps to ensure that we do not objectify and therefore dehumanize one another. We never fully understand one another, so must be open to ongoing learning; it is ethically vital that we recognize the limitations in our apprehension of reality, as they are integral to our quest for solidarity with one another.[28] But there must also, always, be scope for ongoing learning about goodness, as what one presumes to be good, in historical context, can actually be oppressive. For we need to be aware that the very moral benchmarks against which we are prone to judge one another, impatiently, are also necessarily provisional.

Because of these ambiguities, metaphors are rightly picture-painting attempts to grasp what cannot be grasped; they are, in fact, disabled in their attempts to capture God, as God slips through their endeavours. It is therefore necessary and essential to have multiple metaphors, and God as disabled Child is a vital corrective to the dangers of an able-bodied adult.

Communication

It is arguable that this model affects, and indeed helps, how we may view God's communication to us – through the Bible. John Caputo makes the insightful point about the dangers of 'strong' theology:[29] it is theology that insists that it substantially knows the very being of the divine, which he regards as dangerous in its tendency to throw its own weight around and fuel the unaccountable wielding of power – and arguably we see this in relation to holy scripture. For there are those who take its

authority, understood in a certain way, to mean that their interpretations have a particular kind of authority over others and
give them controlling power in many such dynamics – men over
women; straight or cis-gendered over LGBTQI+ people; and
obviously adults over children.

Of course, it can be argued in response that it is only a
strong sense of biblical authority that can *challenge* such
human power-games. After all, God's clear declarations to us
through scripture command us to delimit our own power. And
the language of so much of scripture, steeped in monarchical
power and majesty, imperial power, male power, slavery and
so on, certainly lends itself to an insistence on divine power as
brute power: not to be relativized, but regarded as rock-solid
and imposing. As Ryan Stollar notes, much of scripture is not
appropriate bedtime reading for children, with its casual violence, and even where children are present within it, we are
not adept at engaging with the complexities of the adult matrix
of power or enabling children to navigate it.[30] However, God
the Child, especially God as disabled Child, facilitates a different kind of response, more akin to the 'weak' theology of
Caputo, and which I express in terms of the awesome weakness
of God.[31]

It is this kind of power that speaks to us through scripture:
the power of a child, not incisively articulate, but struggling to
voice dreams, intent, directions; the murmurs and blinks of a
disabled child, trusting that we will learn to interpret the cues,
that we will develop the necessary instincts to make sense of
what is being communicated, building up traditions or bodies
of wisdom to draw on as we engage with the many-voiced
insistences of the Divine Child.

The agency at work is subtle, even if it sometimes screams
with painful clarity. It is a matter of an infant's burbles and
bubbles, which have had to rely on the agency of the humans
who have engaged with ideas, edited and sewn together oral
traditions and the many traces of creative writings, the agency
of humans who have affirmed the canon of scripture, the agency
of humans who have interpreted it, studied it, delighted in it,
wrestled with it and argued with it, wondered at it and worked

with it. All of this gives it its profound authority: the collaboration between the disabled agency of the divine voice and the disabled agencies of the communities of people struggling to make sense of and live out its hopes. For the ability of God the Child, speaking to us through scripture, is not independent of human imagination and community, but very much entangled with it – its dis/ability needs our dis/ability, in a movement of awesome weakness seeking understanding.

In this way, scripture tells us of the truth, the beauty and the goodness of the will of God the Child, but because it is entangled with human imagination and community, there are other things too: struggles between truth and propaganda, beauty and brutality, goodness and destruction, which are all part of the picture of reality, religion and the revelation of God's will, since the ambiguities of life cannot be neatly separated out, and we must indeed struggle with what is being said, rooted as it is in the colonial matrix of adult power – and ableist power.

There cannot be one single mode or posture in our relationship to the cultures we are embedded in. We cannot simply presume that scripture is 'against' culture, as though the tradition is either separate from it or as though it has nothing to give us; God the Child is found in unexpected places, whispering to us, if we have figurative ears to hear – or nerve endings to respond. But neither can we simply be 'for' culture, in its entirety, as though it is not also wounded or captivated by systems that oppress and exclude. We must always seek to be discerning, through engaging with scripture and culture, words and symbols, instinct and self-examination, childlike rage and childlike hope, each ambiguously but authoritatively playing their part in enabling us to discern the inarticulate but incisive wisdom of God the Child.[32]

Fundamentalism, by contrast, imposes certain presumptions on to scripture that are alien to its purpose and nature. In particular, by adopting modern notions of objectivity and inerrancy, and reading the Bible through commitment to these ideas, it re-frames the conversation of scripture as a monologue; it claims there is no struggle, only God's all-powerful voice leaping off the page; it certainly leaves no room for a disabled God who entrusts human imagination and community with significant roles to play in the making and interpreting of scripture. But to me, the fact that people want to make it into an all-secure system of truth-delivery shows not only our insecurities regarding divine truth (which, ultimately, is not the sort of thing to be delivered), but our common unease with patterns of disability in our world – and 'uncontrollable bodies' in which we are a part.

Scripture, instead, testifies to a childlike articulacy of God the Child; a cacophony of sounds and intentions, not all consistent, but a yearning for us to interpret, sometimes grasping hold of their confident assurance, other times delighting in the bubble of wonder that floats out of sight, a fleeting experience of joy that humbles our interpretative adulting. It is such an approach to holy text that helps to make engagement with it a spiritual discipline, not a discipline that limits us, but enables our growth and flourishing. After all, God plays with us through scripture, through storytelling and retelling in a different way, with a new echo, adding layer on layer, while changing some of the bricks of what it constructed previously. God invites us to a desert, a garden, a city, a temple, a tent, a river, a lake, a sea, a mountain and a valley, drawing us into this puzzle, a board game with no obvious end, except somehow, rather than competing with others, we find ourselves sewn together with companions along the way, people of the land and water who yearn for justice and shalom. The rules aren't always clear because sometimes the rule-maker seems to tweak them, even occasionally defy them, and the game goes on – but through it all we learn that we are no puppets on strings, but active agents, friends of the one who sparked the possibility of creation and its renewal.

PS

This part of the book has been concerned with divine power – and I end it here, in an exploration of scripture, because it resembles so incisively the difficult but awe-inspiring nature of God's childlike power, God's chaos-shaped power, like something butterfly-ish distracting us from the normal routines and assumptions of life, power, truth, with the terrifying and amazing revelation that no matter how much we try to entomb the answer, the stones are rolled away.

God's power is not like the sort of thing we imagine.

God's power is not brutish.

God's power is not even adult.

It is playful. It fosters degrowth in a world obsessed with size and scale. It is even disabled in a world longing for bodily mastery, efficiency and victory.

It is its very playfulness, its downsizing, its disability that make justice possible.

It calls out the systems of our world, the colonial matrix of adult power, the imperial economy, the dynamics of power and domination – with a childlike yearning for a different horizon.

Sometimes it does so with screeching clarity but other times it leaves us with traces, glimpses, wisps to follow, through stories that defy capture.

It disrupts and destabilizes an adult world of order and control, with the good news that can't be contained in its playpen; because it is an agency of defiance, a wilfulness of stubborn fairness-seeking, a questioning of adult complacency and insecurity.

It wants to work with me and with you. But if we fail to play the game, it will write on our wall, overturn our tables, and walk through our garden.

Easter hymn

God's awesome weakness greets us on this day.
What seemed like the ending has become the way:
Friday's death was final, Empire did its worst,
burying the story – but the seed has burst!
God's awesome weakness greets us on this day;
what seemed like the ending has become the way!

Sown in the wasteland where new life can't grow,
publicly defeated, making sure we know:
but, when light is dawning, stones and shadows break;
greeting us like Mary, see, the seed's awake!
God's awesome weakness ...

Yet still we'll doubt you – faith is never sealed;
so we'll come with questions: How can life be healed?
Come to us, a stranger, when we walk in grief,
breaking bread to bless us, seeding our belief:
God's awesome weakness ...

(Graham Adams, 2023)
Suggested tune: *Maccabaeus*

Questions

1 What of God not only as Child but as disabled Child? What does this say to you?
2 In what ways may it be helpful, or difficult, to think of God's power as disabled and therefore interconnected with us and our responses?
3 Do you find it helpful to affirm the ambiguous nature of these questions and ideas? Or not?
4 What about the model of the Bible as bearer of God's childlike murmurings, which must be discerned with care? How helpful is it to affirm our necessary involvement in the process?

Notes

1 For example, R. L. Stollar, 2023, *The Kingdom of Children*: *A Liberation Theology*, Grand Rapids, MI: Eerdmans.
2 Graham Adams, 2023, 'Glimpses of God's Dis/Abled Domain: Rising Up against Empire in Small Steps/Huge Leaps', in Jione Havea

(ed.), *Dissensions and Tenacity: Doing Theology with Nerves*, Lanham, MD: Lexington, pp. 167–79.

3 Miriam Spies, 2024 (forthcoming), 'Cripping the Failed Body of Christ', in Néstor Medina and Becca Whitla (eds), *Decolonizing Church, Theology, and Ethics in Canada*, Montreal: McGill/Queen's University Press.

4 Nancy Eiesland, 1994, *The Disabled God: Toward a Liberatory Theology of Disability*, Nashville, TN: Abingdon, p. 102.

5 Eiesland, *The Disabled God*, p. 103.

6 Lisa D. Powell, 2023, *The Disabled God Revisited: Trinity, Christology and Liberation*, London: T&T Clark, p. 44.

7 Powell, *The Disabled God Revisited*, p. 44.

8 Powell, *The Disabled God Revisited*, p. 55.

9 Eiesland, *The Disabled God*, p. 102.

10 Powell, *The Disabled God Revisited*, p. 65. She explains how this is rooted in a kenotic Christology, but not one in which certain divine characteristics were temporarily given up by God the Son but, rather, God was eternally anticipating and open to the receiving of such humanity, p. 66. This builds on Bruce McCormack, 2015, 'Kenoticism in Modern Christology', in Francesca Aran Murphy (ed.), *The Oxford Handbook of Christology*, Oxford: Oxford University Press, pp. 455–6. Incidentally, I almost spoke of God emptying 'herself' here, which would have been no difficulty – but Powell helpfully highlights how models of 'receptivity' can too easily be associated with the feminine, whereas agency is seen as masculine, a sign of heteropatriarchal norms colouring even where inclusive models are sought: pp. 88–9. Even though Powell's and my point here is that receptivity is itself an exercise of agency, not passivity, her caution made me opt for the non-gendered 'their self', which is still transgressive in some respects.

11 Bruce L. McCormack, 2013, 'Processions and Missions: A Point of Convergence between Thomas Aquinas and Karl Barth', in Bruce McCormack and Thomas Joseph White (eds), *Thomas Aquinas and Karl Barth: An Unofficial Catholic–Protestant Dialogue*, Grand Rapids, MI: Eerdmans, p. 124 (as discussed by Powell, *The Disabled God Revisited*, p. 68).

12 Paul Dafydd Jones, 2008, *The Humanity of Christ: Christology in Karl Barth's Church Dogmatics*, London: T&T Clark, p. 225.

13 Powell, *The Disabled God Revisited*, pp. 68–9.

14 Powell, *The Disabled God Revisited*, p. 69.

15 Powell, *The Disabled God Revisited*, pp. 83–4.

16 Powell, *The Disabled God Revisited*, p. 84.

17 Powell, *The Disabled God Revisited*, p. 89.

18 Powell, *The Disabled God Revisited*, pp. 91–4.

19 For example, Doreen Freeman, 2002, 'A Feminist Theology of Disability', *Feminist Theology*, 10(29), p. 77.

20 Marcella Althaus-Reid, 2003, *The Queer God*, New York: Routledge, p. 47.

21 Sarah Coakley, 2002, *Powers and Submissions: Spirituality, Philosophy and Gender*, Oxford: Wiley-Blackwell, p. 21.

22 Powell, *The Disabled God Revisited*, p. 95.

23 Powell, *The Disabled God Revisited*, pp. 96–8.

24 Powell, *The Disabled God Revisited*, pp. 99–106.

25 Graham Adams, 2010, *Christ and the Other: In Dialogue with Hick and Newbigin*, Aldershot: Ashgate, p. 16; Graham Adams, 2022, *Holy Anarchy: Dismantling Domination, Embodying Community, Loving Strangeness*, London: SCM Press, p. 133.

26 Adams, *Christ and the Other*, p. 3.

27 Claire Williams, 2023, *Peculiar Discipleship: An Autistic Liberation Theology*, London: SCM Press, pp. 12, 108, 118.

28 See Anselm Min, 2004, *The Solidarity of Others in a Divided World: A Postmodern Theology After Postmodernism*, New York: T&T Clark, pp. 7–8, who discusses Emmanuel Levinas's 'infinity of the Other' but qualifies it with a 'solidarity of others'; that is to say, while our ignorance of the Other is a basis of our perpetual openness to their identity and well-being, we nevertheless need to build solidarities, however partial and expanding.

29 John D. Caputo, 2006, *The Weakness of God: A Theology of the Event*, Bloomington, IN: Indiana University Press, pp. 7–8, 87–8, 90–1.

30 See R. L. Stollar, 2023, 'Noah's Flood and the Bible's Unseen Children', 14 July, https://rlstollar.com/2023/07/14/noahs-flood-and-the-bibles-unseen-children/ (accessed 07.12.23); R. L. Stollar, 2016, 'Reading Violent Bible Stories Through a Child Protection Lens', *Patheos*, 24 March, https://www.patheos.com/blogs/unfundamentalist parenting/2016/03/reading-violent-bible-stories-through-a-child-protection-lens/ (accessed 18.09.23); R. L. Stollar, 2017, 'Children as Theological Concern and Hermeneutic', *Patheos*, 3 March, https://www.patheos.com/blogs/unfundamentalistparenting/2017/03/children-theological-concern-hermeneutic/ (accessed 18.09.23).

31 Adams, *Holy Anarchy*, p. 109.

32 I have in mind here the different models of H. Richard Niebuhr's *Christ and Culture*, to which I often return when faced with some of the church's arguments about how to be 'against' or 'for' culture, both of which are too one-sided. It is vital to appreciate a rich and complex history of church engagement with culture, which always involves discernment, distinguishing between positive and negative aspects, and seeing how church and faith themselves are also not entirely innocent, so the dialogical process of to-and-fro between religious tradition and wider culture is a challenging but crucial exercise. See H. Richard Niebuhr, 2002, *Christ and Culture*, Boulder, CO: Bravo (original 1952).

PART 3

Whatever God Knows, God is Curious

In Part 1 we revisited the nature of divine omnipresence. In particular, I suggested that God as Child enables us to focus on the smallness of God – that is, the presence of God in the smallest of corners and cracks – and how through such solidarity with experiences of apparent smallness, God's open-handed love is in the midst with us, in all that we face.

In Part 2 we turned to omnipotence, and I argued for the weakness of God the Child, an awesome weakness, which acts like a chaos-event, eliciting effects out of its control. While this is clearly a different model of power from those we are conditioned to expect, being a more playful model of disruption in the midst of dominating systems and structures, it nevertheless represents God's alternative mode of effecting justice, a dis/abled mode that relies on collaborations with other dis/abled agents to build solidarity.

Here, in Part 3, we turn to the third 'omni': God's omniscience or all-knowing nature. I propose that God the Child makes a different model possible – a model of possibility, but essentially a model of curiosity, as the playful, disruptive agency of God ventures after new horizons, pursuing them with an inquisitive vigour.[1] This is a model of God in which God knows the limitations of what God currently knows but has the expansive imagination to appreciate there is more to learn, discover, witness and love. Chapter 7 is where we focus on this image of horizon-seeker, what it means for God to be engaged in the awareness of limitations and curiosity towards new interfaces. Chapter 8 asks what this means for faith. In the same way as Chapter 2 wrestled with the implications of God the Child for our understanding of 'grace', and Chapter 5 explored the nature of 'justice', here I turn to the dynamic nature of faith, an imaginative orientation to reality. It is an energy that relates to theological education – that is, what we think we are doing when we seek to learn *about* God and how, in the light of the God we seek, we are orientated towards a world of unknowing. This relates also to ecumenical relationships and interreligious learning. Then, in Chapter 9, I acknowledge that this reappraisal of our God-models and their childlike implications is something of a 'queer' quest: an otherwise commitment, troubling and destabilizing some of the things we might take for granted. Closed answers, after all, must be questioned; so there must be a deepening of encounter with one another's diverse horizons, a befriending of what is different, including in ourselves, and this is what we see in worship.

Notes

1 Wanda Deifelt, 2021, 'The God-Child Paradigm and Paradoxes of the Incarnation', in Marcia J. Bunge (ed.), *Child Theology: Diverse Methods and Global Perspectives*, Maryknoll, NY: Orbis, p. 88: 'The God-child paradigm invites us to receive God's reign with a childlike attitude: through curiosity and playfulness, through taking risks and posing questions, through seeing life with wonderment, through openness to ask for help when needed, and through a willingness to perhaps not take ourselves so seriously.'

7

God the Horizon-seeker

The wolf shall live with the lamb,
the leopard shall lie down with the kid,
the calf and the lion and the fatling together,
and a little child shall lead them.
(Isaiah 11.6)

'Where then does wisdom come from?
And where is the place of understanding?
(Job 28.20)

God understands the way to it, and he knows its place.
(Job 28.23)

Prayer

Listen. Will you listen? And trust me. I hear you. Praying to
me. It makes me smile and weep. All the languages, caught up
together. Such beauty. Transfixing me in their music. And all
the cries. The yearning. The *yearning*. As well as the thanks-
giving – which is very kind. Of course. But most of all, it's the
hunger that I share with you – hunger for a different horizon.

Your prayers are like a breeze, a gentle whisper in the air,
which help to sustain my flight, as I twitch in the sky, a meagre
butterfly, fragile, straining towards the light, the scent of the
world captivating me till I land where I can, to help to make
connections, however briefly.

Do you see? The horizon beckons, though it seems so far
away. Yet I go there and come back, as though trailing a thread
of possibility, which weaves that place together with here and
now. But it's a struggle, because the thread is costly and the

weaving can break – but each prayer helps to spur me on, stirring courage within me to fly a little more directly. Boldly.

There. Did you detect me tickle the hairs on your face as I came so close, so close? But I know it's hard to believe; surely I should be bigger, stronger, more overwhelming. Not a butterfly-like wisp of wonder. Awe. Majesty in peripheral vision. Distracting you from your routines till you catch a glimpse of that alternative realm, a place so light that it weighs barely anything yet is rich with the treasure of love.

Pray for it. Till it comes closer. As I do. For I long for it. Deeply. As you do. To take root. Here and now.

Inquisitiveness

Again and again in scripture we're given a sense of a tension between one state of affairs and another – the world as it is, on the one hand, and the world as it could be, on the other. The world of wolves preying on lambs or of lions stalking calves, and then the world of the wolf and the lamb resting together or the lion and the calf taking it easy in each other's company. And a little child shall lead them. In fact, might this mean that it is a child who leads the way from one world to the next?

As Walter Kohan explains, such is Paulo Freire's notion of childhood: 'childhood as schooling', representing 'a type of possibility for passage between two worlds'.[1] The point is not that children are schooled by adults, even though they are. Schooling by adults is so often a training to belong in the world as it is. Rather, Freire's point is that the very condition of childhood signifies a state of affairs that can be characterized as 'schooling': a state of possibility. This is the crux: while the experience of adulthood *can* but doesn't necessarily have to be viewed as an ever-narrowing of possibilities, childhood may instead be conceived as a broad vista of possibilities. Of course, it is not always like that – and as we noted in the previous chapter, children's horizons can certainly be limited by the burdens and constrictions imposed on them by the games of the colonial matrix of adult power. Nevertheless, childhood represents a phase of learning with such intensity, as new things about the world are discovered and multiple movements are made towards unknown horizons.

As Kohan also indicates, Freire's commitment to liberative models of education is thoroughly rooted in his memory of childhood, his passionate *curiosity* about the world, not least its stubborn intransigence and the question of what it takes to change things. That is to say, childhood curiosity is so often about a yearning for change.[2] The schooling of the child, for Freire, is not merely a process within the normal routines of life, its *chronos*, but is about being alert to opportune time, *kairos*, which comes as 'gift' but which is stolen from many people;[3] and *that* is the point – this childhood cannot be idealized, because it is still very much subject to the dynamics and whims of systems and relationships that can steal its capacity for alertness to timely possibilities, but – even so – it still testifies to the potential of such a phase of life.

Freire speaks of two kinds of children, who each contribute to this state of possibility: 'connective' children represent the potential for relationship between what is and what can be, between whom we are and what others there are, and 'conjunctive' children signify the process of adding to or transforming, facilitating the growth or generation of something.[4] Cumulatively, as I understand it, childhood signifies this catalytic state: the metamorphosis from one thing to another – not merely once, but as a recurring movement. But for this to be true, actively so, there must be a genuine inquisitiveness: 'What's going on here? Does it have to be like this? How might it be different?'

Childhood, or childness, or childlikeness, is a state of horizon-seeking. Admittedly, becoming aware of strangeness, or of reality worthy of attention, could simply be an experience we stumble into, not intentionally but inadvertently, and that in itself is worth validating; like the chaos-event of serendipity, the surprise encounter that causes a reappraisal of life. But on the whole, what we are dealing with here is the intrinsic inquisitiveness of one who wonders, and wanders, until deeper discovery leads to deeper discovery, and to further questions.

God the Child, then, is deeply inquisitive, because first

answers are not whole answers and God the Child sees through them, with a simultaneous suspicion, wary of adult half-truths and wide-eyed trust, that reality is broader and deeper than the colonial matrix would have us believe.

There is more to encounter, more to embrace, more to empathize with, more to understand, truly understand, and more to love. And the impetus for such inquisitive energy is the desire to engage deeply with how things are in order to hear more intently, experience more deeply, what transformations, if any, are called for.

It is attentiveness, inquisitiveness, motivated by a desire for solidarity, as is inherent for the divine empath.

Incompleteness

Divine inquisitiveness stumbles, however, on the rock of 'completeness'. We saw this in the Introduction: how the 'giant of Completeness' expects God to be complete, self-contained, non-contingent; in other words, *not* on some sort of journey towards new discoveries because that necessarily means limitation and ignorance on the part of the present God.

God can't seek horizons because God is already there. God doesn't need to learn because God already knows. God shouldn't have to be inquisitive about the imperfections in reality because God is already perfectly aware of how things should change. Those are the arguments. But I am not persuaded.

In fact, God the Child might well suspect that such arguments are designed by humans to keep us from asking questions; because these matters are not merely speculations about the inner life of God – they are also inseparable from the dynamics of power between those who don't want other people to ask questions and those who can't help but do so. And if God is already all-knowing, neatly contained within a realm of non-contingence, untouched by the tides and surprises of life in all its fluid complexity, then perhaps people of faith should know not to second-guess, let alone question, the definitiveness of divine authority – nor those who speak for it.

This is John Hull's critical insight in *What Prevents Christian Adults from Learning?* – that churches wary of learning (in a particular sense) energetically preserve the stability and finality of God's knowledge.[5] For if God already knows, then there is a straightforwardness to our learning: it is simply about learning what God knows (captured in scripture) or, a little more humbly, learning to accept our incapacity to know the fullness of things (thus restraining such futile desire). By contrast, other churches and communities allow for genuine speculation, open-ended wondering about God and reality – an open-endedness rooted in the dynamism of God and in the provisionality of our knowledge.

I was both touched and deeply encouraged, at the end of a four-year part-time theology course, when one of our students told me that the three most explosive words they had encountered were my casual but demanding question: 'Does God learn?' It was relatively easy to accept that Jesus learns but they were shaken by the question of God's learning. But at one simple level, if we tell ourselves that learning is a good thing, then it might well be a thing that God does – because God does good things or makes things good. But in perhaps more complex terms, my answer to the question is a confident 'Yes' because I am informed by process theology, which sees God as dynamic, affecting reality but also affected by it; always love but finding new ways to engage in loving a diverse and fluid creation.

Other 'open and relational theologies', such as open theism, make a similar point about God's openness to new futures. There are subtle differences among these theologies about whether God chooses such a humble way of being, giving up the more familiar divine attributes of omnipotence – and perhaps omniscience – in order to show love and maximize our own freedom, or whether it is innate to the nature of God.[6] For me, it is not chosen; it is who God is; it *looks* like a wilful act on God's part because we *assume* God was otherwise all-powerful and controlling, because that is how the weight of history has taught us to conceive of God. But instead, the limitations of God's power and knowledge are inherent to God's nature;[7] for God is intrinsically a relationship-building or solidarity-building God, so does not 'give up' the capacity to control relationships and events, but seeks them out, quietly, gently, longingly.

God's way of being, as horizon-seeker, is to assert only to the extent of demonstrating 'I am the one who is open to ever-new horizons; this is who I am.' It is the assertion of grace, and grace as solidarity: the solidarity to be *with* experiences on multiple horizons, in all their complexity. This self-assertion is also an invitation to us to encounter this very identity – through our own movement towards deeper neighbourliness in solidarity with one another's horizons. That is, for us to know and reflect grace, and grace as solidarity. To know this horizon-seeking God is to know their movement towards deeper encounter; their longing for and seeking of further encounter, richer solidarity, in and among the complexity, pain and potential of everyone's realities. It is a childlike assertion – an audaciously adventurous insistence on movement outwards, to places of unknownness. And it is a childlike invitation – 'Come with me on this adventure.'

This means that every encounter, every relationship, not only each of those far away in a distant galaxy, but even those under our nose, figuratively speaking, is a new horizon; and each is a new horizon for God too, a site and state of potential learning, or schooling, because others' experiences are not God's experiences, so even God must grow into such knowledge and understanding through the patient commitment of encounter, listening, attentiveness, sensitivity, empathy and wonder. And through such movement, metaphorically, God gathers up the connections, or even fragments of them, between the web of horizons: those behind us in forgotten history, those around us in the undiscovered present and those before us in unknown futures. God gathers them and our partial grasps of them; weaves them, knits them together, learning from them and teaching us of them.

On the one hand, this does mean God is incomplete, just as we are; not yet fully Godself, until woven into the struggles, cries and potentials of everyone's horizon, receiving them all into Godself, allowing them to affect who God is, how God is and what God is becoming. (We saw this in relation to the inter-dependence fostered by relationships of dis/ability in Chapter 6.) But on the other hand, because this very openness is intrinsic to who God is, definitive of God's character, it is not as though God 'was' something else and 'will be' something else again, but rather that God is consistently the relationship-weaving God, known through and in the fragility of our knowledge and God's ever-growing understanding of our multiple horizons. After all, a child is not incomplete, but is vitally themselves as a child; they are made in the very image of the God who is always, completely, becoming.

This tension between completeness and incompleteness, between innately being ourselves and becoming ourselves through relationship, is reflected in process theology's other name: *dipolar theism* – which suggests God has two 'poles', one that is unchanging and absolute, another that is changing and relative. This, I think, is a helpful way of framing the dynamism within the life of God: the self-assertion that is not imposing but declaratory of divine invitation and openness, the consequence of which is perpetual receptivity to a fluid and diverse cosmos – and God the Child, horizon-seeker, reflects this interplay, an interplay between the wonder of a child's individuality, worthy of celebration in itself, and the wonder of a child's capacity to embrace newness, surprise and adventurous learning.

God the Child is not afraid of limitation or fragility or divine ignorance, for they are part of the intrinsic identity of the horizon-seeker – not only an open palm receptive to ever more encounters; not only a chaos-event stirring up the exposure of injustices and divisions; but a horizon-seeking Spirit, moving energetically towards unknownness, as a sign of the solidarity-building yearning of the divine empath.[8]

Not yet

It is something that adults often seem to say to children: 'Not yet!' We can be keen to restrain their impatience, whether for understandable reasons, perhaps fuelled by some frustration, or out of an implicit desire to frustrate their hopes – or, more cynically, 'not yet' is a polite but dishonest way of saying 'not at all'. The child's hunger for the new horizon can be so eager, not finding it easy to recognize or accept the obstacles that stand in the way, that we may reluctantly find ourselves saying 'not yet' – but whether for good reasons or bad, it can feel like the unjust judge refusing the widow's persistence in pursuit of justice. 'Don't worry – the time will come!'

No wonder children, and others, find such restraint frustrating in itself – its suppression of eagerness and energy when facing the prospect of a new and exhilarating horizon. The pressure for patience, after all, can be a cunning way of kicking a goal, let alone a ball, into the long grass; to delay and delay again. Bolstering good order. Reconfirming conformity. Denying what is desired. And when we look at the track record of adults, in our respect for the Earth and its peoples, we may well wonder whether 'patience' is a virtue. Shouldn't we instead be barracking and demanding change – and accepting it?

On the other hand, sometimes we give too *much weight* to the 'not yet'. For example, in terms of eschatology and the future-kingdom that is 'now' (but even more so 'not yet') among us, there is an implicit downgrading of the 'now' and a huge investment in the 'not yet': the heavenly banquet when all shall be reconciled. The danger here is that 'now' is given less attention; 'now' becomes a mere waiting room for what really matters; so people's predicaments and suffering *right now* are put into perspective, and into the shade, compared with the glory of what is 'not yet'. In this context, when people demand that real significance is given to the present reality, it can once again be characterized as an impatience for the 'not yet', that the distant future might be brought much more closely at hand – or at least as an impatience for 'now' to be validated and empathized with and loved more deeply. Those resistant to such a focus, and who want us to throw more of ourselves into the 'not yet' of heaven, are not only trying to discipline and restrain such impatience, again, but to turn our attention away from the harsh realities of 'now', to depoliticize our faith by declining to ask questions about current struggles and injustices. In this way, we see how 'not yet' functions within the colonial matrix of adult power: it is a way of instructing childlikeness to get back into its playpen, to focus on trivialities or to grow up and recognize just how hard it is to change things.

It is as though there is an implicit sense that any current agonizing over the kingdom of God is too childlike (or childish), and what is needed is a more adult version: the kingdom that is not yet here – a kingdom of maturity, good sense, respect for rules, calm and measured management of reality, rather than any vigorous yearning for radical transformation. Such naivety is irresponsible, of course.

But I can almost hear the screeching of God the Child, raging against such condescending complacency. The irresponsibility here is the presumption to control how much change is possible. 'Not yet' is seen as a way of holding off access to the genuinely new horizon that beckons us. In fact, the inquisitive God the Child probes our pretension and sees through the sham; they are gathering up the stories from our many past horizons to help them see more clearly, and they're dancing in the direction of something different, something new, chasing it like a kite, caught up in the winds of change; not naively as though pain has dissolved, but fully attentive to the cost of letting things stay the same. For it is all too clear that the prevailing 'kingdom', here right now, is the kingdom of adults, the colonial matrix of adult power, with all its damaging effects, intransigence and distractions – whereas the kingdom 'not yet' here is the kingdom of childlikeness or, as Ryan Stollar calls it, the kingdom of children.[9] That is what waits for us on the horizon – but glimpsed and sensed closer at hand, in the cracks, in disreputable seeds and unclean yeast, growing under our noses and making jubilee possible.

So the movement of God the Child towards ever-new horizons is not the move *from* childlikeness *to* adultness, but is rather the movement into deeper childlikeness; for the (anti-)kingdom that we await is indeed where childlikeness is more fully on earth *as in heaven*. Little ones are given big focus. The unseen and unheard are celebrated. Those small enough to occupy merely the cracks in the current system are brought into the light and cherished, and those presuming to throw their weight around are humbled. It is an anarchic realm, where the seeking of ever-new horizons comes into its own – a landscape infused with empathy, wonder and imagination, so that solidarities between all voices of creation can deepen.

In other words, what is 'not yet' here in its fullness is the realm or reality more fully shaped in terms of the upside-down-ness of God's alternative horizon. The (anti-)kingdom of God the Child.

Hymn: Here is my servant

'Here is my servant in whom I delight,
 who strives to bring justice, who shines as a light';
the child to whom heavens were opened to show
God's blessing revealed that God's kingdom may grow.

'Here is my servant, who won't break a reed
 or quench a dim flame, but with pathos shall lead';
the child to whom heavens were opened to show
God's blessing revealed that God's kindness may grow.

'Here is my servant, a light for the earth,
 who helps people see and gives prisoners new birth';
the child to whom heavens were opened to show
God's blessing revealed that God's freedom may grow.

'Here is my servant, Beloved, shalom –
 the new thing I do as I pitch up and roam';
the child to whom heavens were opened to show
God's blessing revealed that God's movement may grow.

(Graham Adams, 2023)
Suggested tune: Slane

Questions

1 What are you inquisitive about? What intrigues you? What makes you want to know more? And how is such curiosity connected to a longing for change? ('Do things have to be this way?')

2 Incompleteness and God – do the two go together? What makes us resistant to the idea of a God who is 'becoming'? Or in what ways might it animate us – as it animates God?

3 Do you think the expectation of patience is sometimes used to prevent people seeking change – both in the church and in society? How might some childlike impatience be valuable? What is 'not yet' here – a kingdom of maturity or a kingdom of childlikeness in all its fullness?

Notes

1 Walter Omar Kohan, 2021, *Paulo Freire: A Philosophical Biography*, London: Bloomsbury, pp. 128–9: referring to Paulo Freire and Sergio Guimarães, 1982, *Sobre educação: diálogos*, Rio de Janeiro: Paz e Terra.

2 Kohan, *Paulo Freire*, pp. 118–19.

3 Kohan, *Paulo Freire*, p. 129.

4 Kohan, *Paulo Freire*, pp. 125–6.

5 John Hull, 1985, *What Prevents Christian Adults from Learning?*, London: SCM Press, pp. 9–10: fear of confusion keeps adults attached to what they believed as children; p. 37: loyalty is prized; p. 211: 'the assumptions of a uniform orthodoxy, of a content-based revelation, of an instructional and non-learning Jesus'; p. 220. Hull also argues that God is usually regarded as the master, therefore an adult, so to imagine God as being taught could be seen as demeaning by sending God 'back to school'.

6 We encountered this debate in relation to 'kenotic christology' in Chapter 6 – see p. 130.

7 Thomas Jay Oord calls it 'essential kenosis'; that is, though it looks as though God has self-emptied, the reality is that God already was, and

is, essentially 'emptied' of such power. See Thomas Jay Oord, 2019, *God Can't: How to Believe in God and Love after Tragedy, Abuse and Other Evils*, Grasmere, ID: SacraSage Press, chapter 1; and Thomas Jay Oord, 2015, *The Uncontrolling Love of God: An Open and Relational Account of Providence*, Westmont, IL: InterVarsity Press, chapter 7.

8 Hull, *What Prevents Christian Adults from Learning?* Hull also affirms this dynamic movement of God from God's knownness to what is unknown; 'God as the perfect learner is also the perfect changer' (p. 226), being open to new experience, learning through it and thereby being/becoming not quite the God that God was previously.

9 R. L. Stollar, 2023, *The Kingdom of Children: A Liberation Theology*, Grand Rapids, MI: Eerdmans.

8

Faith as Imagination

Now the Arameans on one of their raids had taken
a young girl captive from the land of Israel, and she
served Naaman's wife. She said to her mistress, 'If only
my lord were with the prophet who is in Samaria!
He would cure him of his leprosy.'
(2 Kings 5.2–3)

After three days they found him in the temple, sitting among
the teachers, listening to them and asking them questions.
(Luke 2.46)

Parables

The kingdom of God is like an orange circle with a blue smile
and green legs, holding hands with a purple square with yellow
teeth. It may look like a weird orange alongside a purple alien.
But it's not. It's a picture of a dream that makes friends with a
sadness.

Or it's like a Lego house with a swimming pool and the big-
gest table for parties and a petting zoo and a climbing frame
and a gaming room and a mountain with a river and a rainbow
and some horses and some chocolate and a craft table and a
quiet room and a fridge to put the picture of the dream and
people who aren't all the same colour and some of them have
autism and some of them are vegetarian and some of them are
disabled and some of them have a sad face and some of them
are dancing and some of them want to be on their own and
some of them like to play with marbles.

Or, I know! I know! It's like this big sheet of paper, a blank
piece of paper, and there are lots of crayons and pens and

paintbrushes around the edge, and people get to make this huge mural together, and nothing they do is wrong and everyone loves it.

Faith/imagination together

The young nameless girl sees what is possible. If only. If only Naaman were with the prophet. But he isn't. Not yet. But she sees how that possible future would make things so different. She has the imagination to see. Or we can call it faith. She trusts: things would be different if ...

It takes a child, even a girl captured against her will, trafficked far from home but still somehow capable of seeing the alternative history and future. Her memory has not been wiped. So the parallel path of a different future – even one for her oppressor – is offered by her. Such intense generosity on her part. A nameless child – though, of course, she had a name, but we are not told it. Perhaps it was taken from her, perhaps she was given a new one, perhaps the narrator didn't think her name was what mattered – or perhaps they're making a point: that wisdom comes from those deemed unworthy of being named. In any case, the arguments seem so casual, as is the stating of her trafficked identity; noted so matter-of-factly, laying bare the ease with which a child's value is both minimized but how such minimization is simultaneously the means through which God reveals truth. Faith comes in mustard-seed-sized packages, unwanted but capable of moving mountains.

So too the 12-year-old Jesus is lost; but after three days (a hint of resurrection?) his lost-ness turns into something deeply revelatory: he was in the midst of teachers, both listening and asking questions. This is a mark of his faith, which adults did not have the imagination to envisage. Engaged, attentive, in the throes of debate, seeking deeper understanding, probing not with his immediate peers, but they are becoming his peers – because with him, we all become peers to one another. Children and adults together.[1]

The relationship between faith and imagination is obviously

complex, and within religious communities we are prone to see other religious people as those who are lost, while we may lack the imagination to grasp how they belong within our own debate. For instance, I recognize that I lack the imagination to understand and appreciate how some people can insist that the Bible must be entirely historical; it bewilders me; I cannot step sufficiently out of my own world to make sense of theirs. Similarly, they would find it hard, I think, to imagine the validity of my perspective; they seem to struggle with the legitimacy of imagination itself as a means of revelation, believing instead that only historical facts can be the basis of reliable faith. To me, this peculiarly modern insistence, informed by science's quest for facts, involves its own act of imagination; for they 'imagine' that biblical narratives are best understood as historical events. The prospect of human make-believe entangling with divine revelation is too chaotic and slippery; so they maintain a line that they claim is derived from scripture itself, that its historical objectivity is fundamental. To me, in contrast, the notion of any text's objectivity, let alone a religious text, and its stark distinction between historicity and imagination, is too fantastical to make any sense.

In secular realms, too, we find a comparable wariness of imagination: policymakers and many politicians seem increasingly disparaging of subjects and courses that are seen as economically non-productive, and these are primarily in the humanities and arts; in contrast, the good drivers of growth, like maths, science, engineering, technology and computing, are celebrated. This is depressing and bizarre on so many levels. First, because creative subjects are good for the quality of life in ways that economic growth can never comprehend; second, the interdependence of creativity and productivity is overlooked; and, third, this denigration of imagination is also a suppression of empathy. Of course, not all adults are like this, and certainly not all of the time, but the pressure within our political economies to reduce education to outcomes that can be recognized in economic terms, and to package education in ways that will maximize such 'rationality', is to wage war against childlikeness and its innate imagination.

Meanwhile, within such pockets of childlike imagination, resistance to the machine is kept alive. And faith has a crucial role in inspiring this. Alternative futures are possible, as the slave-girl recognized, precisely because, even when we're subjected to dehumanizing forces, there is a cry within us that cannot be entirely silenced. Stacey Gibson speaks of imagining as 'an act of liberatory adventure since it feels borderless, boundary less, and free from the constructs that bind. To imagine is to transcend.'[2] No wonder Paulo Freire sees the spirit of 'infancy' as 'revolutionary' – 'its curiosity, its restlessness, its delight in questioning, its not being afraid to dream, its desire to grow, to be creative, and to bring about change'.[3] There we see how imagination and restlessness belong together: an urge to see through – and break through – walls that bind; an energy that resists passivity; an audacious belief, even despite the evidence, that something else is possible.

In those effervescent terms, the Bible cannot be merely a history book, no matter how thrilling history books may be; nor even a moral guide, a series of prescriptions; rather, it is so much more: an interplay between the contingencies and possibilities of human histories, and faith-infused imagination – because its good news is that God is deeply entangled in the mess and ambiguities of the human psyche and social life, with revelation emerging when people think, wrestle, pray, play, wonder, wander, struggle, dream, debate, weep and yearn. Some of its most inspiring passages and messages are acts of divine/human imagination, with God the Child spurring us into beautiful re-framing of what *is* and re-imagining of what *could* be. As G. K. Chesterton said: 'Fairy tales are more than true – not because they tell us dragons exist, but because they tell us dragons can be beaten.'[4] So too for Freire: such a celebration of childlike imagination is not about idealizing childhood, since much of 'the bounty of the child's universe is not accessible to all children', but childhood is 'this will of transforming the world so that not only certain lives are real lives of joy, of curiosity, of love'[5] – but everyone's. The honour of *Bambino permanente* (permanent child) was thus bestowed on Freire in 1990, because he lived out this revolutionary spirit of childlike re-imagining.

To have faith, then, is both to see the world as it is, which in itself requires imagination, to enter empathetically into the cracks and small spaces of a vast, fluid and diverse world, building solidarity among the different, and to imagine its renewal, even its transformation. It is God the Child who flies this kite alongside us, dancing, skipping and singing, while also lamenting, sighing, bawling.[6] Childlike imagination is the audacious freedom, as yet unrestrained by the colonial matrix of adult power – the audacious freedom to be boldly alert to what is and what might be, in all its smallness, all its containment and all its hidden potentiality.

Learning/teaching together

What does this mean for how religious communities, including those engaging in formal theological education, foster environments of learning and teaching? For Freire, the revolutionary infancy that is restlessly curious, 'playfully throws itself into building a pedagogy of the question, which learns and teaches to ask questions'. As Kohan explains, 'It even ventures to ask itself "what does it mean to ask questions?"'[7] This is what adults most need: 'a childlike revolution' marked by 'a permanently … questioning state'.[8] Communities of the Question!

Of course, there are risks in centring the experience and model of childlikeness. As a mode of being, it may be exploited by bullies, 'giants' and the colonial matrix of adult power, exacerbating its vulnerabilities and treating its students as empty vessels, void of wisdom or agency. The bullies declare: 'We are in charge here!' But it is precisely because of such a system, its patterns and habits, that the mode of childlikeness that I am celebrating is necessarily a revolutionary mode, a questioning way of being – and this cannot be fully fostered through the bravery of individuals, valuable and impressive as they are, fighting against the matrix, but should be an educative culture in which coalitions of childlikeness are encouraged.[9]

Education needs to be attentive and hospitable to the childness that is available to us all, if we can recover it; to love our childness, for all its excitement, restlessness, wonder and questioning.[10] In this respect, the idea of 'brave space', as opposed to 'safe space', is very helpful.[11] We need safe space that helps people to feel secure, which may be especially important for people from marginalized groups, but to address difficult issues, to probe norms, assumptions and systems, brave space is needed, extending beyond safety, enabling risk-taking, even if there is some stumbling and awkwardness in the process, as there will be. Where a safe space would help people agree to disagree, a brave space could push through to 'controversy with civility'.[12] Where a safe space allows people to challenge *by choice*, in brave space we are asked, if we choose *not* to be challenged: What is the impact of that choice?

There we see that questioning takes us further, beyond safety and into childlike courage. In quite a different context, considering the nature and shape of mission, Cathy Ross explores the 'unfinished agenda' of how we think about, educate and foster mission practice, recognizing that the greatest single 'unfinished' aspect of this is racialized in the light of colonialism.[13] That is to say, our questioning must take us further with regard to the norms and legacies of Whiteness, how colonial mindsets play out in mission education and the way mission is exercised. Within her argument, she highlights the work of bell hooks, for whom 'eros' is critical for good education. As Ross puts it, it is 'an energy or passion that propels us towards learning as an adventure'. In hooks's terms, as a motivating force it can 'invigorate discussion and excite the critical imagination',[14] fostering relationship, co-learning and co-creation of knowledge.

In light of this imaginative and revolutionary restlessness, committed to questioning and courage, how might we generate good theological education together, informed by the agency of God the Child who energizes our own childlikeness? While there are so many models we might address or develop, I offer simply three dimensions. I see these as the 'arts' of theological education, which are all defined by our orientation towards God's (anti-)kingdom, the alternative social horizon that we pursue but which is close at hand.

The first is discernment: our task is to co-learn the art of recognizing the (anti-)kingdom; to help one another to discern it, to declare it and to delight in it. Crucially, any such discernment requires sensitivity and collaboration – both of which involve empathetic imagination; not merely rational thought, but an alertness that enables us to make connections between what we know and new data that comes our way when we engage openly with the world, with our tradition, with one another. The making of connections is not straightforward because we may have a certain idea of what the kingdom is, informed by our grasp of the historical traditions given to us, and then we come across an aspect of life that is new to us; we are not sure what to see or do but childlike imagination helps to keep alive the capacity to see it, to tune in with it, despite its difference. Discernment, therefore, requires sensitivity – the ability to be attentive to the quiet voices within our own story and in the world at large, and to allow them to intermingle, to see if they are at all singing the same tune in a different key or with a distinctive structure, so freeing us to spot the kingdom if it is there.

Such sensitivity also calls for collaboration; the readiness to align with others who are also seeking the kingdom, though they may not have that language or all of the same presuppositions about it – and they may well have had their experiences, insights and practice suppressed by the colonial matrix of (adult) power. As Willie James Jennings notes, Jesus would often engage with 'the crowd',[15] an awkward mix of people who might otherwise not share space, but it is only through such a new solidarity – among the different – that good discernment and good practice can genuinely be fostered. Only such an approach can undo the 'mastery, possession and control' that have dominated theological education, its Whiteness having determined its content, parameters and mode,[16] and the 'self-possessed man', identified by Mike Higton, who has been used to being centred.[17] The crowd, by contrast, becomes a space in which we mutually discern, recovering voices that have been under-heard, allowing the kingdom to look less like the colonizing kingdoms and more like the alternative horizon where reconciliation is at last possible.[18] As David Clough identifies, this means talking much more about the connections between theology, Whiteness and 'race', undertaking more research, addressing the recruitment challenges (through mentoring and learning from good practice) and re-evaluating the content.[19]

Ross refers to Ibribina's story, told by Simon Barrington-Ward.[20] She was a prophetic, illiterate woman leader and trader in Niger in the 1880s, who sought to create a 'fellowship of the unlike' – people whose differences and dissonances meant they should not be able to collaborate, but they did, inspired by her witness – Black and White, rich and poor, strong and weak, mutually seeking a new heaven and new earth. Though the colonial missionaries tidied up her work, and even shut it down, her witness is of a new possibility, a subversive and restless imagination in practice. It is also the sort of horizon envisaged by Eve Parker in her critique of trust in theological education,[21] since more trust is too easily given to the 'received' power and legacy of the usual suspects, whereas an alternative is not only possible – it is what we should actively seek. But first it must be discerned, hidden in the cracks of church and mission history, or further at large, through collaborative conversation in our nudging towards ever-braver spaces.

This process of discernment, however, also requires awareness of 'epistemic injustice', as Parker argues;[22] that is to say, White westerners have presumed that their 'ways of knowing' are intrinsically superior. So *how* we know and *what* is known both need to be revisited, through 'epistemic disobedience',[23] to redistribute not only knowledge but power, in order for the conversation of discernment to be genuinely more inclusive – and troubling. For Anthony Reddie, the 'decentring' of Whiteness goes together with the 'decolonizing' of the curriculum, requiring a 'subversive and systematic shift to the margins'.[24] Arguably, while different from Blackness as we explored in Chapter 3, childness can speak to this epistemic disobedience or subversion in education, asserting other ways of knowing and creating space for different voices. As Parker states, 'The injustice of the colonization of the mind is one of the gravest injustices that has been committed against the majority world'[25] – and it is one undertaken by the colonial matrix of *White, adult* power.

Second, then, and very much entangled with the first art of theological education, we should seek to embody this vision, to 'spread the table' of such inclusivity and potential, to reflect it (however imperfectly) in our liturgical, educational and missional culture. As Paul Joshua Bhakiaraj argues, in the context of the church, children are integral to this; for as he puts it, 'it takes a whole church (which cannot be conceived without children and young people) to raise a Christian.'[26] In other words, we are not talking about 'how best to raise Christian children' as such, but how people are formed in communities and, since childlikeness is inherent to the church's vision of the alternative social horizon, children and childlikeness have a key part to play. Of course, the risk here is that they are instrumentalized,[27] reduced to useful tools in the task of furthering a larger project. But the centrality of children is more fundamental than that: it is to align their very being with the reign of God, in the sense that the 'kingdom of God' is the 'kingdom of children'.[28] Ryan Stollar's book of that title argues for children as agents, advocates, campaigners, leaders in their own liberation and in changing the world. Children and childlikeness are therefore not simply 'useful'; in fact, they are much more destabilizing than they are useful – because they present us and our complicity with the colonial matrix of adult power, with a systematic problem: How different are our structures and habits from those of the 'upside-down kingdom' that is represented by the centring of children?[29] So too Reddie interrogates the structures of power within UK theological education, to see how mastery, patronage and, conversely, indecency and transgression are navigated, managed and judged; asking what topics (or ways of knowing) are compulsory and what are optional; whether 'reflexivity' is affirmed and Whiteness is decentred.[30]

What this means for theological education is far-reaching. This is not simply a question of whose voices we seek out, in order to discern more fully the presence of the (anti-)kingdom in the world at large. This is also about the dynamics, patterns (including the ways of knowing) and cultures that we inhabit when engaging individually and collectively in the task of discernment. What is required for us to rediscover ourselves as 'children' of this alternative social reality, this new horizon that we claim to pursue but which we hold at bay through our unimaginative perpetuating of existing dynamics and hierarchies? After all, no matter how much we say we desire it, our historic systems and norms divert us away from it – and it may be a kind of childlikeness, like that of Freire, that beckons us back on track, its 'eros' or passion for adventure leading us through difficult terrain, across wild and unruly seas[31] and into the possibility of a new heaven and new earth, where Ibribina lives.

Helpfully, though, this challenge reminds us that we ought not to expect to be the perfect embodiment of the horizon, because we continue to be entangled in the colonial matrix even as we desire its undoing – and what matters is that we honestly own that ambivalence. We seek to do education in ways that playfully generate co-learning/co-teaching, where people's stories and insights are woven into the web of meaning and life ('reflexivity'), as contextually and inter-contextually as possible, as we struggle to engage with the myriad experiences, questions and possibilities, wrestling openly with scripture, its own imaginative interplays and the different futures that beckon to us. At its best, such decolonization 'is opening things up, reappraising existing truths, offering contestation and challenge from the margins, and moving away from rigid certainties around what constitutes the canon of knowledge'[32] – all signs of the childlike pursuit of a new horizon.

Third, then, theological education must be active space, pursuing that vision of transformation rather than merely talking about it; allowing practice and struggle to inform its reflections, and its reflections to spill over into anticipatory action, daring to imagine that new worlds might be lived. This requires partnerships, even messy ones, because no educational community lives in a vacuum and no theology can be done in a silo; so we help to form one another – the teachers themselves being continually formed and reformed, in collaboration with students – and we test out our imagined futures in present engagement with the questions and commitments of real communities. Those partnerships might be educational or civic or interreligious or global; they might be temporary or experimental or permanent. They should reflect the intermingling of people preparing for formal roles with a wide range of other ministries; they should come out of, and speak into, intergenerational concerns and enthusiasms; they should be intersectional, anti-racist, decolonial as we seek out the kingdom where the first are decentred and the last are centred. In a sense, what this means is a commitment to 'make new friends' and build communities of deepening friendship, through which the adventure may proceed with restless but mutually supportive determination.

Between these three arts of theological education – discerning the alternative horizon, embodying it even partially and pursuing it in partnership with others – we see that theology itself is not best understood as a set of ideas, but as a conversation or debate, a process, an adventure of discovery and unlearning, a movement towards undiscovered territory, a mapping out and re-imagining of things. These are deeply childlike in their openness to questioning and possibilities; it is a profound curiosity that interrogates the world as it is and the world as it might become.

It is, as I hope is evident now, God the Child who animates this theological adventure, rushing ahead and calling us over the brow of the hill to see a different landscape stretched before us: 'Come and see!'

Intra/interreligious conversation

What about the implications of childlike imagination for engagement among Christians and among those of different religious traditions?

First, of course, it's worth noting that not everyone in these relationships would affirm God the Child, either in other traditions or in Christian community. God the Child is used to this! The sidelining of their voice or minimizing of the questions they pose would be familiar enough, but the remarkable thing about God the Child, if children's experience is at all indicative, is that they somehow manage to endure and survive such belittlement;

after all, empathetic solidarity with the little in all sorts of ways and places is a defining mark of this divine/human interplay. Ivone Gebara, building on the work of Paul Ricoeur, identifies four broad areas in which many children experience their needs and desires not being met,[33] within this colonial matrix of adult power – 'the need to be protected, cared for and nourished; the desire to have power; the desire to possess; [and] the desire to be recognized'. The desire for power is about agency, the freedom to act and have some ownership over the trajectory of one's life in the social realm; the desire to possess is about the dignity of possessing clothes, shelter, food and more; and the desire to be recognized is about being seen, validated, valued. In each of these respects, structures and systems act as impediments – and of course, religions play their part in this.

Conversations about children, like any hypothetical or actual conversation about God the Child, would be conflicted, even if well-meaning – within churches, ecumenical contexts and interreligious environments. As such, the restless and imaginative questioning of God the Child would be seen as precocious, audacious, subversive, but it is, in any case, a liberative metaphor and story.

Second, sometimes it is evident that particular traditions (within a single religion and in the conversations between different traditions) presume to be the 'grown-up', viewing others somewhat condescendingly, as though they are immature children. The more ancient the tradition the more it may behave in this way, whereas those traditions that arrived later on the ecumenical or interreligious scene may either incidentally find themselves performing as, or consciously relishing the role of, adolescent newcomer – the 'upstart' presuming to question the norms and wisdom of the 'parental' traditions, or perhaps older 'siblings'. If this is the case, God the Child has an important role: to disrupt such dynamics; after all, even adults continue to be children, and children can be adult-like. (For example, Freire speaks of the 'double existence' of childhood joy and the challenge to be prematurely adult;[34] and Rohan Gideon criticizes the simplistic adult/child dichotomy[35] – which we discuss further in Chapter 9.)

The question of different traditions viewed through the prism of adultness/childness makes me wonder whether I happen to see my own Congregational tradition as childlike, affirmingly. Though I am certainly happy to acknowledge the frailties of its ecclesiology, frailty – or weakness – in itself is not a problem; rather, it is a legitimate indicator of childlike vulnerability. What matters is whether we own those frailties and accept that other traditions have gifts to offer – which has indeed been the ecumenical approach of Congregationalists, celebrating the potential for Christians to be united by a model of diversity that can transform any indifference, condescension or resentment into patterns of equity and mutual recognition. More assertively, however, there are other features that point to a valuable childlikeness: the Congregational affirmation of the small (the local church being valid in itself, rather than needing blessing from an external 'larger' body); the commitment to relationships of mutuality, as all are equal in church meetings where the mind of Christ is sought under the guidance of the Spirit (an audaciously anarchic claim to the revelatory power of relationships of equality, thereby giving legitimacy to voices that might otherwise be overlooked or belittled); the daring notion that individual churches might reach different conclusions in light of their faithful attentiveness to what the Spirit is saying in particular settings (a gloriously chaotic freedom!); and a spirit of dissent that challenges the abuse of power or any pattern of domination by social systems and state agents (speaking up for freedom of conscience, freedom of religion, the dignities of 'the little person', in solidarity with all who feel the weight of overbearing giants).

Of course, other traditions also witness to God the Child, with particular features resonating with various childlike enthusiasms, such as dressing up, lighting candles, moving furniture, raising arms to sing, ritual and so on. Indeed, Congregationalists will certainly not all be conscious that their tradition reflects such a divine agency; this is part of the paradox and mystery of God's power as chaos-event, subtle and in need of discernment, present in the cracks and across borders. At their best, though, ecumenical conversations and relationships can be animated by

– and can pursue discovery of – God the Child, the imaginative horizon-seeker whose quest enables deeper relationships of mutuality and interconnectedness. The church, in all its diversity, witnesses to, seeks to embody and pursues this alternative social reality where the smallness, weakness and curiosity of God the Child comes on earth as in heaven.

So too in interreligious relationships: there will be disagreements, which arguably require brave space, not merely safe space; there will be idealization of children as people essentially in need of protection rather than as agents capable of teaching adults; there will be uncertainty about the notion of God the Child whose identity feels too insubstantial. But that will surely not be the whole story.

Marcia Bunge identifies various things that, in a religiously plural context, children can learn, embrace and act on – the need to respect one another as human beings, made in God's image, so safeguarding one another's freedom; the need to love and serve one another, in part by being attentive to diverse beliefs and practices; seeking justice together in pursuit of the common good; being free and able to share one's story of faith, owning the distinctiveness of one's identity together with the commonality of particular values.[36] However, this is still largely about what children can learn, whereas God the Child shows us the childlikeness of the divine agent, who calls us towards an alternative horizon. There are Hindu traditions, for instance, that especially cherish the stories of Krishna's childness; they are held with particular affection, even though the infant Krishna is quite mischievous; in fact, it is his mischievousness that is said to evoke a loving response in humanity.[37] As I wrote elsewhere,[38] Kristin Johnston Largen's work highlights how Christians have lessons to learn through the question of divine playfulness. Catherine Cornille also argues for the centrality of hospitality in interreligious encounter[39] – that, in effect, each tradition understands the significance of hospitality, perhaps sees it slightly differently, is able to receive the stories, similarities and dissonances of one another, and can collectively appreciate that no one tradition is ultimately the host; rather, we must learn to be guests of one another and of God – or, in the context of non-theistic traditions, of transcendence, the Other, reality itself.

Perhaps we should think of it as a children's festival – a brightly coloured array of traditions in encounter with one another, with some spaces where play and creativity are accentuated, others where serious discussion is enabled, still others where reflectiveness, spirituality and worship are fostered. It is a space in which people learn to be friends – not that all will be smooth, all differences will be perfectly handled, all truth will be heard and understood, but that the (anti-)kingdom on the horizon comes a little closer through empathetic acts of imagination, adventure and curiosity.

This is the work of God the Child – (not) the Father, (not) the Son (nor) the Holy Spirit; and yes, the brackets are intentionally mischievous, capturing the ambiguity and identity-confounding nature of the Child who is and isn't comparable to more familiar ideas, but playfully, quietly and boldly, simultaneously something less and more. We turn to the paradoxes of this – its mess and mystery – in our final chapter concerning the queerness of the quest.

Hymn: Let us dream

Let us dream of a future of fairness,
Let us dream of a world at peace,
Let us dream of a feast for all people –
may our dreaming never ever cease!

Sing together, play together,
dare to question what's impossible!
When we're used to catching nothing,
show us nets becoming full!

Let us go – out beyond shallow waters,
be like children who dare to leap,
let us go where our courage will take us:
new things happen where our hope is deep.

Let us dream of a future of fairness,
Let us dream of a world at peace,
Let us dream of a feast for all people –
may our dreaming never ever cease!

(Graham Adams, 2022)
Suggested tune: *Give me oil*

Questions

1 What do you see as the strengths and weaknesses of seeing faith as imagination?
2 How do you respond to the vision of theological education that prioritizes these 'arts':
    i Discerning God's (anti-)kingdom, wherever it may be found – which requires more diverse relationships with all who share in such discernment?
    ii Embodying God's (anti-)kingdom, however imperfectly – which requires humility on our part, while spreading the table with a passionate spirit of adventure?
    iii Pursuing God's (anti-)kingdom in partnership with others, so making friends with different movements seeking overlapping goals?
3 How might it help ecumenical and interreligious relationships to imagine God the Child inspiring and calling us to deeper engagement with people/places of smallness, building a creative solidarity of the diverse and focusing on the alternative social horizon where all are reconciled?

Notes

1 See Rohan P. Gideon, 2021, 'Soteriology and Children's Vulnerabilities and Agency', in Marcia J. Bunge (ed.), *Child Theology: Diverse Methods and Global Perspectives*, Maryknoll, NY: Orbis, p. 104: a 'rooted solidarity of the caring community', which requires attentive listening by adults, intentionally fostering 'a deeper intergenerationality'.

2 Stacey A. Gibson, 2017, 'Sourcing the Imagination: Ta-Nehisi Coates's Work as a Praxis of Decolonization', *Schools*, 14(2), pp. 266–75.

3 Paulo Freire and Antonio Faundez, 1989, *Learning to Question: A Pedagogy of Liberation*, trans. Tony Coates, New York: Continuum, p. 140.

4 Or: 'Fairy tales do not tell children that dragons exist. Children already know that dragons exist. Fairy tales tell children the dragons can be killed.'

5 Walter Omar Kohan, 2021, *Paulo Freire: A Philosophical Biography*, London: Bloomsbury, p. 138.

6 Dirk J. Smit, 2021, 'Reimagining Hope *with* and *like* Children', in Bunge (ed.), *Child Theology*, pp. 211–15, highlighting children's 'crying with sorrow' and 'laughing with joy'.

7 Kohan, *Paulo Freire*, p. 142; citing, there, Freire and Faundez, *Learning to Question*, p. 37.

8 Kohan, *Paulo Freire*, p. 142.

9 Kohan, *Paulo Freire*, p. 143: Freire was aware of the 'hostilities' of the system; in the face of them, he asserted that 'the future is not a given datum, a destiny, a doom'; Paulo Freire, 1994, *Pedagogy of Hope: Reliving Pedagogy of the Oppressed*, trans. Robert R. Barr, New York: Continuum, p. 112 (translation modified).

10 See Kohan, *Paulo Freire*, pp. 146–7.

11 See, for instance, from an educational context, https://blogs.kcl. ac.uk/activelearning/2020/10/28/safe-spaces-and-brave-spaces/; or in the world of business, https://kapriconsulting.ca/blog/2023/03/21/creat ing-brave-spaces/ (both accessed 20.07.23). In particular, see Brian Arao and Kristi Clemens, 2013, 'From Safe Spaces to Brave Spaces: A New Way to Frame Dialogue Around Diversity and Social Justice', in Lisa M. Landreman (ed.), *The Art of Effective Facilitation: Reflections from Social Justice Educators*, New York: Routledge, pp. 135–50.

12 Again, see https://blogs.kcl.ac.uk/activelearning/2020/10/28/safe-spaces-and-brave-spaces/ (accessed 07.12.23).

13 See Cathy Ross, 2022, 'Newbigin Annual Public Lecture', 2 July, https://seedbeds.org/2022/07/05/newbigin-annual-public-lecture-2-july-2022-by-dr-cathy-ross/?s=09 (accessed 20.07.23). In the context of children's formation, Valerie Michaelson also argues for decolonizing

and anti-racist processes, materials and culture: 2021, 'A Decolonial Approach to Formation and Discipleship', in Bunge (ed.), *Child Theology*, pp. 172ff.

14 bell hooks, 1994, *Teaching to Transgress: Education as the Practice of Freedom*, New York: Routledge, p. 195.

15 Willie James Jennings, 2020, *After Whiteness: An Education in Belonging*, Grand Rapids, MI: Eerdmans, p. 151.

16 Jennings, *After Whiteness*, p. 6.

17 Mike Higton, 2023, 'Beyond Theological Self-Possession', in Anthony G. Reddie and Carol Troupe (eds), *Deconstructing Whiteness, Empire and Mission*, London: SCM Press, pp. 14–18.

18 David Clough, 2023, 'Deconstructing Whiteness in the UK Christian Theological Academy', in Reddie and Troupe (eds), *Deconstructing Whiteness*, pp. 27–32: Clough outlines how White this context has been.

19 Clough, 'Deconstructing Whiteness', pp. 34–6.

20 Ross, 'Newbigin Annual Public Lecture'; Simon Barrington-Ward, 1999, 'My Pilgrimage in Mission', 'Newbigin Annual Public Lecture', *International Bulletin of Missionary Research*, 23(2), p. 61.

21 Eve Parker, 2022, *Trust in Theological Education*, London: SCM Press.

22 Eve Parker, 2023, 'Re-Distributing Theological Knowledge in Theological Education as an Act of Distributive Justice in Contemporary Christian Mission', in Reddie and Troupe (eds), *Deconstructing Whiteness*, p. 41.

23 Parker, 'Re-Distributing Theological Knowledge', p. 42, using the concept from Walter Mignolo, 2009, 'Epistemic Disobedience, Independent Thought and Decolonial Freedom', *Theory, Culture & Society*, 26(7–8), pp. 159–81, 161.

24 Anthony G. Reddie, 2023, 'Dealing with the Two Deadly D's: Deconstructing Whiteness and Decolonizing the Curriculum of Theological Education', in Reddie and Troupe (eds), *Deconstructing Whiteness*, pp. 54–5.

25 Parker, 'Re-Distributing Theological Knowledge', p. 48.

26 Paul Joshua Bhakiaraj, 2014, 'The Whole Household of God: How Children Can Deepen Our Theology and Practice of Missional Ecclesiology', in Bill Prevette et al. (eds), *Theology, Mission and Child: Global Perspectives*, Oxford: Regnum, p. 129.

27 This is a danger highlighted by D. J. Konz, 2021, 'Reforming Mission with Child-Attentive Theology', in Bunge (ed.), *Child Theology*, p. 191.

28 Gideon, 'Soteriology', p. 97; developed further in R. L. Stollar, 2023, *The Kingdom of Children: A Liberation Theology*, Grand Rapids, MI: Eerdmans.

29 Bhakiaraj, 'The Whole Household of God', p. 130.

30 Reddie, 'Dealing with the Two Deadly D's', pp. 62–6.

31 The image of 'wild and unruly' seas, chaos or the Spirit is depicted by Upolu Vaai in his call for the oceans: https://ptc.ac.fj/a-call-for-the-ocean/ (accessed 20.07.23).

32 Reddie, 'Dealing with the Two Deadly D's', p. 68.

33 Ivone Gebara, 2021, 'Children's Experiences of Evil in their Multiple Worlds', in Bunge (ed.), *Child Theology*, p. 54.

34 Kohan, *Paulo Freire*, pp. 126–7.

35 Gideon, 'Soteriology', p. 98.

36 Marcia J. Bunge, 2014, 'Faith-Formation in an Inter-faith World: Passing on the Faith to Children Amidst the Realities of Religious Pluralism', in Prevette et al. (eds), *Theology, Mission and Child*, pp. 203–12.

37 Kristin Johnston Largen, 2011, *Baby Krishna, Infant Christ: A Comparative Theology of Salvation*, Maryknoll, NY: Orbis, pp. 50–61.

38 Graham Adams, 2019, *Theology of Religions: Through the Lens of Truth-as-Openness*, Leiden: Brill, pp. 69–70.

39 Catherine Cornille, 2008, *The Im-possibility of Interreligious Dialogue*, New York: Crossroad, pp. 177–9, 197–210.

9

The Queerness of the Quest

'Where is the child who has been born king of the Jews?'
(Matthew 2.2)

*'For a child has been born for us, a son given to us;
authority rests upon his shoulders; and he is named
Wonderful Counsellor, Mighty God, Everlasting Father,
Prince of Peace.'*
(Isaiah 9.6)

Queering the dichotomy

'Queer theology' is obviously concerned with many different matters – not only sexuality (which I indirectly consider in the next section), but questions of indecency,[1] and is increasingly applied to a wide range of topics and questions beyond those that are less immediately obvious. For instance, Queer Religious Identity is not as such about the place of sexuality within religious identity, but is far more about the queering of such identities, their boundaries and precepts, especially in the light of religious diversity, and identifying how sacredness is to be found in the scandalous nature of tradition and its sense of divine presence.[2]

For the purposes of exploring the implications of God the Child, there are three particular ways in which queering is relevant – first, the challenge to the binary or dichotomy of adult/child identities; second, the prevalence and significance of liminality (thresholds or edge-places) – in particular, the horizons to which God the Child leads us out of perpetual curiosity; and third, the question of friendship, especially friendship that defies the strictures of social divisions.

Behind these, there is the point I have made a few times now: that the different liberative movements of Black, Disability and Queer theologies function in a similar way within this overall argument, since they each show us that, in order to effect liberation for the respective groups and their interrelatedness, one part of the picture is to see God in those terms, as Black, Disabled and Queer – and so with children too. God the Child is a necessary aspect of the full humanization and liberation of children.[3] What this means is that the Adult God cannot presume to do all the talking; the Child must be heard – in fact, greater weight needs to be given to the child metaphor.

Rohan Gideon draws attention to the biblical ambivalence regarding children:[4] often not validated in themselves but as signs or means of something else – signs of the covenant or of their parents' faithfulness; whether a woman bears children is a measure of her; they are also reduced to economic agents, they are traded as entities, so are dehumanized; and yet at the same time, Jesus is shown to regard them as pivotal – and there are other examples: the boy David defeats Goliath; Naaman's slave-girl; Samuel and Jeremiah, the child prophets. In some of these entanglements between adults and children, children's own status is not the question – they are simply ciphers for adult games; in others, they are crucial; sometimes they do adults' work for them, other times they implicitly represent the invitation for adults to grow *down*![5] In these complex interactions, we see the instability of the dichotomy between Adult and Child – whether in terms of a dichotomy concerned with power, status, knowledge or agency. The dynamics are certainly not straightforward.

This insight is not especially radical in itself: we know from so many aspects of life that dichotomies are often false and binaries are widely questioned. But there is arguably a particular queerness to the destabilizing of God's adultness, because the notion of God as Adult is so ingrained in us.

To make the point, a little diversion: in Chapter 3, I argued that God the Child subverts monarchy – again, it is not the only theological movement to raise such questions and, conversely, I am sure that some people may be drawn to God the

Child without accepting the conclusion that monarchy is problematic. After all, these issues – in the ambivalent and chaotic criss-crossing of multiple commitments – are not clear-cut. But at the very least, what we see is the queering of monarchical assumptions: a child *born* king (Matthew 2.2), who is also declared king (however mockingly) *on the cross* (Luke 23.38), is obviously not a straightforward king; and the child envisaged by Isaiah – clearly a child but also proclaimed 'Everlasting Father' – is not within our familiar parameters. To the extent that there is kingship in the divine, it would appear to be unrecognizable. So can we say that, to the extent there is adultness, it is best understood as unrecognizable?

Patterns of power; patterns of status; patterns of control; patterns of authority – they are simultaneously 'higher' than our ways (Isaiah 55.8–9) and more humble, more subversive, more uncharacteristically dissident; in fact, only 'higher' *by virtue of* their subversiveness. This is why God is innately anarchic, destabilizing the very notions projected by us on to them. This is why, a little playfully, I suggest God as Child is (not) the Father, (not) the Son (nor) the Holy Spirit; the brackets being ambiguously, queerly, pertinent: for it is clearly in relation to the parenthood of God's nature, and therefore the Trinity as a whole, that the perpetual childness of the Divine raises issues.

How can God be both parent and child? Of course, the Trinity itself affirms this. But my argument for God as Child is not confined to the 'second person'. Nevertheless, what the Trinity does is allow us to speak of paradoxes within the divine life – and there are indeed multiple paradoxes in our theological storytelling: between transcendence and immanence, eternal life and crucifixion and so on. I am suggesting, though, in line with other liberative movements, that greater weight is to be given to certain metaphors over others, not in order to dismiss the prevalent and dominant ones, but in order to make a point about God's solidarities with various experiences. It is the very interplay between God as Adult and God as Child that is a queering of our assumptions; God the Adult 'becoming' Child, not merely by way of incarnational theology, but as a reconfiguring of our theological attention. The result is that the adult/child dichotomy is destabilized, the child being given more attention by virtue of its very littleness, its belittlement, its overlooking, and the parent is humbled, brought down from their throne, while the child is fed, nourished, cherished, centred – and indeed liberated. The Adult God grows downward, as Jesus urged us to do, as we too rediscover the perpetual childlikeness of God.

Trinitarian theology is queered as a result of re-framing it in the light of God the Child – for this is God as open palm, God as chaos-event, God as horizon-seeker. Or in other words, God the open palm, a child's palm, attentive and empathetic to whatever the world throws at it, even 'be-child-ing' their own 'parent-ness' in solidarity with all little spaces. This is God whose presence is small enough, everywhere, to be in solidarity with all who are belittled. And God the chaos-event, be-child-ing the 'weakness' of the Christ-event, its agency evoking the agency of others, an emerging solidarity of all-comers. This is God whose power is awesomely weak enough to spark possi-bilities among all kinds of people – struggling within, disabled by and seeking to transform the colonial matrix of power. And God the horizon-seeker, be-child-ing the Spirit with adventur-ous questioning, discerning, seeking to embody and pursuing the alternative social reality, the (anti-)kingdom. This is God whose knowledge is incomplete enough to motivate and fuel such deep curiosity towards the multiple horizons of experi-ence, gathering them up in empathetic neighbourliness.

Horizon-seeking as love in liminal spaces

I have been describing the movement towards horizons in terms of childlike adventure and have argued that empathetic attentiveness to one another's horizons is well represented by childlike curiosity. The image of the horizon is another way of speaking of the alternative social reality, the (anti-)kingdom or Holy Anarchy – which is both out of reach and close at hand, a paradoxical phenomenon because it is simultaneously impos-sible and vital, something that cannot insist its way into being but is nevertheless found in the cracks, in sites of unlikeliness, evoking new possibilities.

This is all very well, but of course I haven't discussed a particular feature of horizons: they move. As we move towards them, they move away from us. This raises the question about the term itself – is it actually helpful or does it add to the bewildering impossibility of the task that surely God the Child does not have the power or knowledge to overcome? How we answer the question depends on how we conceive of horizons and how we understand our imagination in reaching out towards them.

On the one hand, yes, a horizon is something we will never reach; in which case, the effect can be disempowering, even though our curiosity will never be exhausted because there will always be more to encounter. On the other hand, there is no single horizon, but rather a plethora of horizons, because even different people standing near one another do not see entirely the same horizon, and of course multiple people are located differently in relation to many different horizons, some of which are where we are located already – which brings us to a different realization.

In certain respects we stand on other people's horizons and they stand on ours. This does not mean that some of us are already perfectly located on the alternative social horizon of God's (anti-)kingdom, because there will always be a sense of its paradoxical state – among us and ungraspable, since it defies control but is nevertheless alive and well in unlikely places. Even so, the awareness of multiple horizons, and the fact that we can be located on one another's, illuminates for us a double lesson. On the one hand, we can be answers to one another's prayers, by virtue of being alert to what others are seeking, so building ever-deeper solidarity among one another; neither precociously imagining that any group of us is the exact fulfilment of others' horizons nor minimizing the capacity of people to play our part in the engendering of justice, peace and healing. We are, after all, connected in the web of life – an awareness to which children can be especially sensitive.

Pertinent to this sense of a web of connections, Roseline Olumbe discusses the five systems within which children grow, as identified by Urie Bronfenbrenner's ecological systems theory.[6] Microsystems are the immediate settings with bi-directional relationships between the child and others (home, school, church); mesosystems are the interactions between those settings (for example, the relationships between a child's teachers and parents); exosystems are wider structures where the child is not directly involved, but structures have a bearing on them (neighbourhood, parents' workplaces, mass media); the macrosystem is marked by cultural structures and forces (socioeconomic status, ethnicity, location, ideologies); and the chronosystem are the changes over time, such as life transitions and historical events. Together, these bioecological systems impact the well-being and flourishing of a child. Olumbe identifies these in order to bring them into dialogue with *Ubuntu*, the African principle that our humanity is shaped through relationship with others – and collective responsibility for children's welfare and fullness of life is vital. These systems, enhanced by the notion of *Ubuntu*, also reflect what I have been saying about horizons: some are much more immediate to us, some are distant; some are more under others' control than ours; some are indistinct and some are all too clear. But in essence, not only are children raised in the context of such interweaving horizons and environments, they may also demonstrate for us the childlike curiosity of seeking out strange and unknown horizons.

This childlike capacity to embrace the quest for one another's diverse but interweaving horizons is a sign of God the Child among us, like a butterfly evoking responses in us as we find ourselves empathetically attending to those who are different, and even building solidarity – brave space in which individuals may flourish without being conformed; instilling self-love in contexts generating self-hatred.[7] But this notion of horizons interacting with one another also sheds light on another lesson we may learn.

On the other hand, there is the sheer liminality of horizons, because they are spaces both on the edge and clearly in between one state and another. This is why liminal spaces are significant in queering, as spaces of 'christic creativity' – that is, created by

Christ and where further transgression can germinate.[8] They refuse to be confined and they offer the possibility of transition.[9] As discussed by Carson et al., the dynamism of liminality is represented by Bruce Reed's oscillation theory[10] – which, as Stephen Roberts helpfully summarizes, is 'to do with movement between inner and outer worlds as we negotiate the sacred and secular divide'.[11] So for our purposes regarding horizons, when one horizon-seeker encounters another's horizon – or, rather, the space/place/setting that was horizonal to the seeker but 'everyday life' to the other – an experience of oscillation occurs; that is between one's sacredness and another's, one's secularity and another's, one's identity and another's, one's horizon-seeking and another's. That is to say, encounter presents us with new experience, some of it affirming, some unsettling, some safe, some dangerous, some loving, some threatening.

In this spirit of encounter, much as we identified God the Child as Black (in Chapter 3) and disabled (in Chapter 6), so they are also queer. As others have argued, God or Christ is queer, or indecent;[12] and here I relate this specifically to God as Child. They are a child moving towards the horizon of their own identity, alert to the unconforming and 'transgressive'[13] nature of their desire – in their case, because their desire breaks the bounds of more limited notions of love. They are having to discern when and how to come out as public witness,[14] to reveal their self-identity, attentive to diverse contexts – in some, recognizing that the experience may be relatively safe and accepted, while in others it may be unsettling, risky, dangerous. So there will be antagonism, struggle and fragility; these are fairly easy to name in writing, as expressions of the vulnerability of Jesus' message,[15] but that naming should not be taken casually in the real world, where anti-LGBTQI+ prejudice, persecution and violence are rife. God the Child as queer therefore represents further solidarity, with marginalized and transgressive groups.[16] But the dynamics will be different in multiple environments, where one struggle intersects with others, whether Blackness, socioeconomic class, disability or neurodiversity. In fact, the respective bioecosystems of different contexts mean that the queerness of God the Child will be affected in varied ways:

bearing the pain while seeking to be themselves, which may require defiance and 'pride' as protest, or may be subtle, gentle, under-the-radar. Their solidarity with other children experiencing such a wide variety of realities will be deep, whether in the margins between systems, or enabling them to move towards the centre, or on the move towards unrealized horizons; weeping where there is weeping, rejoicing where there is freedom and justice.

The role of God the Child in all such encounters between one's horizon and another's, one's experience and another's, is first to inspire them to happen at all; to prompt people to enter more fully into the understanding of one another, or at least into understanding how difficult it is to understand each other, acknowledging the provisionality of our grasp of another's horizon. But, second, God the Child's role is to increase the chance of neighbour-loving habits and legacies. The horizon-seeking God is in their own process of such encounter, oscillating between inner and outer worlds, discovering their own self and their relatedness with others, between one person's multiple ecosystems and the interactions between different people's ecosystems; a relational God actively engaged in fostering relationships of mutuality, justice, wholeness, without ever imposing or even determining outcomes.

Befriending at the edges

Following on from the image of the horizon as the place of encounter, we can perhaps imagine God the Child seeking friendship. Previously I suggested that Jesus may be understood as the friend, even the best friend, of God the Child, in addition to its embodiment and kite-flyer, but here I am suggesting that it is the very horizon-seeking of God the Child that makes them a seeker of friends.

In Queer theology, Jesus is seen as unclean friend, one who challenged norms of the family and religious purity codes,[17] placing himself in settings of uncleanliness, in among those deemed dirty because of religio-political judgements, so befriending across boundaries. God the Child, then, is immersed in the mess, in sites of liminality, on the edge; connecting with those who are not allowed to be, or may not want to be, 'clean' according to the vested interests of the colonial matrix. They seek out such transgressive friendship, which cuts across all kinds of loyalties – those of class and status, those of gender and sexuality, those of ethnicity and culture, those of dis/ability, those of neurodiversity, those of age. The befriending of God the Child is a subversive act.

In *Holy Anarchy* I discussed the story of Mary meeting Jesus in the garden, at first not recognizing him but then, on hearing her name, realizing who he is. I suggested that this meeting place is in effect a meeting place between two worlds – the dominant world in which we cannot recognize the presence of new life, because it is so different from what we are conditioned to expect, and the alternative world, which beckons us into a new future. To me, this is the basis of worship – or we could even say it is the *very nature* of worship: we bring into encounter with one another our lives conditioned by the world as it is, the world that prevails and in which new possibilities are mocked or marginalized, and the world as it might be, a distant horizon that somehow is closer to us than we expected. Worship is the very encounter between these two, inviting us to bring our honest lament, our struggle, even our despair, but also our hope, our desire, our yearning, and God receives it all and works with it all, like an open palm, like a chaos-event, like a horizon-seeker: receiving, stirring and pursuing.

In such encounters, God the Child 'makes friends' with these diverse, awkward experiences; God the Child receives them empathetically, as the divine empath with an ever-open palm; God the Child is animated by them and animates us in response, like a chaos-event, stirring, prompting, making new things possible; and God the Child moves towards new horizons, curious and change-making, engaging in ever-deeper understanding of our own horizons and, through this understanding, builds solidarities among us, in pursuit of grander, deeper and more neighbourly horizons at which the alternative social reality comes on earth as in heaven.

Through such befriending of experiences, in all their diversity, pain and potential, God the Child also inspires us to make friends – with God and with one another; with neighbours near at hand and neighbours further away; with those we find it easy to understand and those who make us curious, whether warily or enthusiastically. At these places of encounter, liminal places where strange encounters happen, not least in worship as we enter into one another's worlds more fully, our curiosity is nourished and our adventurousness is stimulated – and we find ourselves becoming friends with unlikely people. This is, after all, the 'fellowship of the unlike', as we saw in Chapter 8. This is an alternative social reality, which we are pursuing. This is a strange new world, marked by brave spaces, where encounters between neighbours and enemies become sites of transformation – against the odds.

Of course, it is not always like that. After all, the colonial matrix of adult power and its other variants (White power, male power, able-bodied power, straight power) has this peculiar hold over us, making us apparently addicted to the world as we know it; the world obsessed with growth and consumption; the world wreaking havoc on its ecosystems of life and diversity; the world fuelling suspicions and divisions. This matrix of power holds sway and makes it very difficult for friendship to emerge – especially friendship among the unlikely. Friendships, we have been taught, however implicitly, ought to be between people with things in common; it would be too queer to be otherwise. But God the Child rises up against this system, this matrix, this interlocking set of norms – and dares to dissent and build alternative friendships, cutting across ethnicity, gender, sexuality, class, dis/ability, neurodiversity and age. And at its best, worship is such a place of encounter – an otherwise space.

I was struck how, when some people saw one chapter title in my book *Holy Anarchy*, they imagined that it said 'the horizontal God', not the 'horizonal God' – but actually both are intertwined, not least in worship. It is space as though at a horizon, where different experiences encounter one another, but it is also a site where we see God is horizontal in relation to us, not over and above but in the midst with us, and where God is at work helping us to be more horizontal with one another, more equal, more just, more *Ubuntu*, more mutual; for worship is where co-creators meet, befriend, collaborate and move.

In worship we become friends – which is not to say that all animosity, resentment, jealousy, angst or suspicion dissolve, but that we are invited to make friends with our own struggles rather than deny them; we are invited to make friends with our own questions rather than convert them into answers; we are invited to make friends with the versions of ourselves that we either hold at bay or yearn to become; we are invited to make friends with the questions and quirks of one another; we are invited to make friends with the church's frailties, not to let them be, but to understand that some will remain even as others are transformed; we are invited to make friends with the past, even as critical friends wrestling with it, and with the present in all its diversity, and of course with alternative futures in which things are seen to be really quite different.

God the Child leads the way towards deeper friendship, making friends with us more wholly and inspiring us to make friends with ever-new neighbours – and all creation.

Hymn: Rainbow God

The rainbow tells God's wonder-news,
evoking childlike awe;
bright glow confronting us with truth,
shy faintness, wanting more;
an arc of light from local star
that waves its way within,
refracted through the stuff of life –
this world-upturning grin!

It hangs to mark past violence,
illuminates our lies:
for no one sees it quite the same
or looks through others' eyes.
Its vivid palette scattered wide
acclaims diversity:

it flows from God, the Uncontained,
who loves such vibrancy!

And if this vision's honed in Christ,
pulsating with God's light,
then let's reflect and not distort
such empathetic sight:
not judging outlook, tone or tribe
by lies of purity,
but every wavelength given space
and Black lives' liberty.

In Christ, our rainbow-God made flesh,
we'll covenant again
and build communities that change
through neighbours' cries of pain.
We'll hear the cosmic chorus sing
of life's immense array
and learn to live within the whole,
the rainbow-loving way!

(Graham Adams, 2020)
Suggested tune: *Kingsfold*

Questions

1 How might things be different if we gave more weight to God the Child than God the Adult?
2 What do you make of the horizon-seeking and transgressive God as one who leads us into deeper encounter with one another's diverse experiences, in the creativity of liminal spaces?
3 Why do you think 'befriending' might be a potentially transformative understanding of worship – in terms of God's befriending of us, showing us how to befriend each other and enabling us to befriend different aspects of ourselves?

Notes

1 Interestingly, Yin-An Chen's critique of 'indecenting' takes a turn to the *micro*-political – that is, in effect to the smallness of the subject-self, one who is constructed through spiritual practice, capable of enacting resistance to capitalist accounts of identity; this is one area where it would be interesting to develop further conversation beyond the parameters of this book. See Yin-An Chen, 2022, *Toward a Micro-Political Theology: A Dialogue between Michel Foucault and Liberation Theologies*, Eugene, OR: Pickwick Publishing.

2 See Paul Hedges, 2012, 'Guanyin and Identity: The Image of a Subversive Religious Icon', *Religion and Culture*, 13(1), pp. 91–106.

3 On their humanization and liberation, see Rohan P. Gideon, 2021, 'Soteriology and Children's Vulnerabilities and Agency', in Marcia J. Bunge (ed.), *Child Theology: Diverse Methods and Global Perspectives*, Maryknoll, NY: Orbis, p. 102; and R. L. Stollar, 2016, 'Towards a Child Liberation Theology', *Patheos*, 7 April, https://www.patheos.com/blogs/unfundamentalistparenting/2016/04/towards-a-child-liberation-theology/ (accessed 18.09.23): 'they are not only to be formed but to be imitated … they are not "just" children but representatives of Christ.'

4 Gideon, 'Soteriology', pp. 98–9.

5 Graham Adams, 2022, *Holy Anarchy: Dismantling Domination, Embodying Community, Loving Strangeness*, London: SCM Press, p. 112. I include my hymn in which there is the exhortation: 'May adults grown downwards'.

6 Roseline Olumbe, 2022, '*Ubuntu*: Conceptualizing Community for Children in the African Context', in Rosalind Tan, Nativity A. Petallar and Lucy A. Hefford (eds), *God's Heart for Children: Practical Theology from Global Perspectives*, Carlisle: Langham Publishing, pp. 75ff.: she refers to Urie Bronfenbrenner, 2009, *The Ecology of Human Development: Experiments by Nature and Design*, Cambridge, MA: Harvard University Press.

7 Lisa Isherwood, 1999, *Liberating Christ: Exploring the Christologies of Contemporary Liberation Movements*, Cleveland, OH: Pilgrim Press, p. 104.

8 Tom Driver, quoted in Robert Goss, 1993, *Jesus Acted Up: A Gay and Lesbian Manifesto*, New York: Harper & Row, p. 127: regarding inbetween-ness; and Isherwood, *Liberating Christ*, p. 105: regarding 'Christic creativity'.

9 Liminality is discussed much more in Timothy Carson et al., 2021, *Crossing Thresholds: A Practical Theology of Liminality*, Cambridge: Lutterworth Press.

10 Carson et al., *Crossing Thresholds*, p. 4: referring to Bruce Reed, 1978, *The Dynamics of Religion: Process and Movement in Christian Churches*, London: Darton, Longman & Todd.

11 Stephen Roberts, 2023, Book review: 'Crossing Thresholds' *Practical Theology*, 16(2), May, p. 312.

12 For example, Marcella Althaus-Reid, 2003, *The Queer God (God the Homosexual)*, London: Routledge.

13 Isherwood, *Liberating Christ*, pp. 102–5.

14 Isherwood, *Liberating Christ*, p. 103.

15 Isherwood, *Liberating Christ*, p. 103.

16 Isherwood, *Liberating Christ*, p. 109: 'an embodied friend who revels in the ongoing discourse, loves the challenges, and celebrates the joy of connection'.

17 William Countryman, 1989, *Dirt, Greed and Sex: Sexual Ethics in the New Testament*, London: SCM Press.

Conclusions

Following the Child

Then Abraham fell on his face and laughed, and said to himself, 'Can a child be born to a man who is a hundred years old? Can Sarah, who is ninety years old, bear a child?'
(Genesis 17.17)

So Sarah laughed to herself, saying, 'After I have grown old, and my husband is old, shall I have pleasure?' The LORD said to Abraham, 'Why did Sarah laugh, and say, "Shall I indeed bear a child, now that I am old?" Is anything too wonderful for the LORD? At the set time I will return to you, in due season, and Sarah shall have a son.' But Sarah denied, saying, 'I did not laugh'; for she was afraid. He said, 'Oh yes, you did laugh.'
(Genesis 18.12–15)

Laughter

Can't you see, God, how funny it is? Extremely old adults bearing a child. Of course they would laugh!

Imagining the exertion. Imagining the labour. Imagining themselves running around after it. Imagining themselves trying to remember everything they need to do.

Imagining themselves standing next to the parents of their child's friends, and talking about events, experiences, expectations – how different they would be.

The thought of childness coming into the least likely place is, well, ridiculous.

Surely you can see.

Yes, of course I see – because I am laughter; I am joy; I am dancing. The prospect of Childness bursting to life in the midst of such profound adultness is, well, amusing for me too.

But it's vital: not just in this moment, but again and again, the call for Childness breaks in, and adults must learn to embrace it –

To welcome the Child, the divine/human Child, the one who brings disruption, who asks questions, who evokes joy, surprise, wonderment – but who also understands sadness, who weeps with you tenderly, who rages against injustice, screaming out against the intransigent forces of control and division;

To welcome the Child, with their openness to new experiences, the chaos that they bring and cause, their adventurous pursuit of new horizons;

To welcome the Child who dares to show that impossible things just might be worth expecting.

So if you know it's funny, as well as a little frightening, why ask why it was that Sarah laughed?

I'm God the Child! I love to ask good questions – even if I don't have all the answers!

The gaps

This is unfinished. It is still growing. Its potential is also, no doubt, unrealized; at least it will not be fully realized for some time – if ever fully realizable.

This is obviously true in the sense that, as a book trying to make a new path by walking it, I am only talking it in some tones not in others, and on some interfaces instead of many others. For instance, there is much more work to do in engagement with the theology of childhood, children's spirituality and development, and with the Child Theology Movement – and I certainly hope that others will help to flesh out these many connections and more. My focus, though, having come from slightly different beginnings, has been more explicitly 'theopolitical'; that is to say, I am concerned with the way, in a context of a colonial matrix of power, particularly adult power, the possibility of God the Child has been suppressed and its potential insurgency remains unawakened.

This project is unfinished, therefore, not only because it is a small work taking small steps in particular directions, opening up various unanswered questions, leaving trails of adventure unexplored, but also because its very theme is necessarily concerned with unfinishedness. It is not that I regard children as unfinished, because they are whole, in themselves – but as we heard Paulo Freire insist, they represent a state of possibility. For him,[1] it is as though there is a childhood waiting in all sorts of environments – in schools and communities and in the wider world, 'waiting to be awakened'. In fact, there are 'many childhoods' – which, on the one hand, is a life-affirming possibility but, on the other, he starkly warns us: 'Society pressures us to kill this child within, but we must resist … this child who leads me to love life so much.'[2] The task of giving life to God the Child, who was alive before us in any case, remains unfinished because there are so many stronger forces seeking to silence it.

The thing is: God the Child is dangerous.

Of course, children are not only dangerous – and even in the sense that I intend it, it is a rising up against structures and patterns of injustice, so it is a positive danger, at least for the sake of those belittled by the prevailing system. But this brings us to the recurring question of idealization: am I always selecting those aspects of childhood that reflect what I believe God to be like and editing the less desirable realities? Each time I come back to this critique I confess to some bewilderment because our adult images and models are also deeply selective – and the childhood dimensions I focus on are not naïve or innocent, I hope, but engaged in the mess, struggle, questions and possibilities of creation.

For example, in response to an earlier presentation of the prospect of God the Child, one person said to me, 'You must have a well-behaved child.' This question arrested me because I did not think that I had given any impression of the congruence between childness and being well-behaved – in fact, if anything, I thought I had focused on the disruptiveness of the kind of childness I have in mind, and I would say that our God is not well-behaved, but is disruptive, subversive, anarchic, turning things upside-down. Even so, the question was profound because it demonstrated how this notion of God as Child may be *received*; of course, I don't mean received by everyone, but perhaps by *many* people – as though it is a naïve project, conjuring up images of a sweet, innocent, cosseted and compliant God.

To be as clear as I can: first, from the political end of my argument, God the Child exposes and confronts the colonial matrix of adult power, refuses to play by its rules, dances to a different tune, one of solidarity in the midst of all who are belittled, as a divine empath, an attentive and sensitive soul in touch with the deepest pain and loss of others' realities; and they evoke chaos, a playful pursuit of justice, drawing us away from obsessions with size, scale, expansion and extraction, towards degrowth, the beauty and connection of smallness, in partnership with others whose agency feels weak or disabled by these systems, making possible alternative movements; and they imagine alternative horizons, beginning in a deep readiness to understand others' horizons, within themselves and beyond, until there is an interdependent interweaving and the renewal of all creation.

Second, to support this, when Jesus places a child in our midst to prompt us to think differently, to turn around and to upend our assumptions, we should not picture a well-kempt, well-behaved, polite and manipulable child, but one more like a street child, streetwise and unnerving, or from a so-called 'chaotic home', or a child whose energy does not conform to the patterns of adult power – fragile, yes, but defiant. And we could add so many different characteristics, depending on where we are located, but which would subvert our expectations – whether Black or Brown or East Asian or Pacific (and so on), or neurodiverse, or physically or intellectually disabled, or queer, or poor … or any combination of every possibility, but certainly not one who fits in with the norms of the prevailing powers. And then this child, who shows us the way into

God's alternative realm, an (anti-)kingdom or Holy Anarchy, may be presumed to give us a glimpse of God as Child. I recognize, though, within such a wide range of connections and intersections, I have not addressed several of them very much – intellectual disability, neurodiversity, class and many of the interweaving realities; but I have begun to point to the relationships between God's solidarity and all such experience, and to argue that there is more work to do here, trusting that some of these threads will be pulled, following new trails of identity, questions and possibilities.[3]

It is worth noting too that I do not differentiate between the different *ages* of childhood (infancy, toddler, primary school-aged, teenager). Perhaps I should make such distinctions, to make the particular assertions of childlikeness better defined, even if overlapping, because I appreciate that the phases of childhood can be quite starkly different. But the phases of adult life can also be significantly distinctive, yet we do not think to distinguish between them when conceiving of God's adultness: God is simply Adult. In any case, childhood phases are notoriously difficult to separate from one another, because children change at different rates – and I am wary of such measurements, not least because God as Disabled Child throws the notion of developmental milestones to the wind.[4] More fundamentally though, I am not making an argument for God progressing through the stages of childhood; rather, that childness in all its richness and complexity is a vital way of understanding God in their wholeness. God can be simultaneously infant and teenager, dependent and strident, inarticulate and incisive; God can be a toddler playing with building-bricks and a toddler dismantling towers; God may be bawling, impatiently waiting for us to learn what they are communicating to us, and argumentative; God can be adventurous and quiet; laughing and sleeping, mischievous and curious and so on.

Finally, I do not always articulate my reasoning when I move between different terms – God the Child, divine childness, childlikeness, as well as human childness and, to a lesser extent, childhood. I accept that this may be frustrating, but these ideas necessarily overlap and nourish one another, without always being distinguishable. While I was conscious of choosing one or the other, I admit that I did not state why. Nevertheless, God the Child is not the same as a human child; after all, divine childness is metaphorical and analogical, expressing the dynamic interplay between 'God' and 'Child'. I am exploring the childlikeness and childness of both – where 'childness' suggests something more constitutive, definitive of identity, whereas 'childlikeness' allows for a little more distance, the possibility that childness is 'performed', so adults may be child-*like*, but we should not forget that we never lose a fundamental child*ness* too. For we who are adults are called to become like little children. Why? Because God is!

The God the Child Creed

We believe in God the Child
Big enough to be everywhere
But always small enough to be in the places we can't see, or
    won't see –
The overlooked places
With belittled people
And the creepy-crawlies of creation
Giggling with joy
Weeping with sadness
Really aware of what's going on – more aware than the
    grown-ups –
Seeing through the lies
And holding out an open hand to touch it all
A hand that becomes dirty in the soil
In the mess
In the pain
And a heart that aches with the dream that things could change
We believe in God the Child
Bold enough to say 'This is me'
To spark possibilities
Like a wind of chaos
Crying out that things aren't fair and the Earth is groaning

Overturning the tidy rooms where we learned to keep things
in boxes
Bringing the giants and bullies down to earth
Making the dragons inside us turn their fire into breath
And raising up the little people
Hearing their stories
Giving room for questions to be asked
But weak enough to know others' weakness
Building connection
Dreaming dreams
Planting and watering and building
Together
Even when our efforts aren't what we had hoped
And things still get us down
We believe in God the Child
Who has faith that is tiny
As small as a mustard seed
But it gets in the cracks
And it takes root
And its roots start to break the walls that limit our imagination
And it dares to dream –
See the horizon stretching before us
And calling us –
And we follow the Child
Deeply curious about the very smallest details
Knowing that we don't know
Seeing that we can't yet see it all
But trusting that we can join our horizons together
With all sorts of people
And the many cries of creation
Until we remember
It all started with smallness
In weakness
And divine curiosity
Loving
Life
Loving
What could be

Hymn: Hark the herald …

Hark! The herald angels sing,
interrupting everything:
God, whose glory fills the earth,
pitched a tent of humble birth!
Where we long for new release,
where we hunger after peace,
bear the pain and count the cost,
numb with grief for all we've lost,
    Hark! The herald angels sing,
    interrupting everything.

Hark! A voice begins to dare:
in the wilderness prepare!
Raise the valleys long ignored
and disrupt each mighty lord:
Where the lust for power consumes,
where faith dances to such tunes,
squeezing out the room for grace,
leaving only manger-space,
    Hark! A voice begins to dare:
    in the wilderness prepare!

Hark! Your God is here at play,
living life another way,
interrupting grander schemes,
sparking stranger kinds of dreams:
where God's spirit comes to rest,
bringing hope to all oppressed,
where the captives are set free,
sign at last of jubilee,
    Hark! Your God is here at play,
    living life another way.

(Graham Adams, 2020)

Notes

1 See Walter Omar Kohan, 2012, *Paulo Freire: A Philosophical Biography*, London: Bloomsbury, pp. 149–50.

2 Paulo Freire, 1985, *The Politics of Education: Culture, Power and Liberation*, Hadley, MA: Bergin & Garvey, p. 197.

3 For example, see Claire Williams, 2023, *Peculiar Discipleship: An Autistic Liberation Theology*, London: SCM Press; and Molly C. Haslam, 2012, *A Constructive Theology of Intellectual Disability: Human Being as Mutuality and Response*, New York: Fordham University Press.

4 See Graham Adams, 2023, 'Glimpses of God's Dis/Abled Domain: Rising Up against Empire in Small Steps/Huge Leaps', in Jione Havea (ed.), *Dissension and Tenacity: Doing Theology with Nerves*, Lanham, MD: Lexington, p. 170.

Index of Bible References

Index of Names and Subjects